WHAT HAPPENS WHEN WE PRAY FOR OUR FAMILIES

Evelyn Christenson

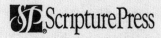

Amersham-on-the-Hill, Bucks HP6 6JQ, England

ISBN 1 872059 72 4

Unless otherwise noted, Scripture quotations are from the *New American
Standard Bible* © the Lockman Foundation 1960, 1962, 1963, 1968, 1971,
1972, 1973, 1975, 1977. Other quotations are from the *Authorized (King
James) Version* (KJV); *The New King James Version* (NKJV), © 1979, 1980,
1982, Thomas Nelson, Inc., Publishers; the *Holy Bible, New International
Version* (NIV). Copyright © 1973, 1978, 1984, International Bible Society.
Published by Hodder & Stoughton Ltd. Used by permission.

Produced and Printed in England for
SCRIPTURE PRESS FOUNDATION (UK) LTD
Raans Road, Amersham-on-the-Hill, Bucks HP6 6JQ by
Nuprint Ltd, Station Road, Harpenden, Herts AL5 4SE.

DEDICATION

To my wonderful extended family who travelled this sometimes arduous but always victorious road of prayer with me.

To Sally Hanson, the other half of my ministry, for her nineteen years of untiring and humble seeking of God's wisdom for the uncharted path and awesome doors He was opening to us.

To my faithful board members for never ceasing to pray for my family and me as we have needed them so desperately.

But, most of all, to my Heavenly Father, who has performed all these incredible things for my family in answer to those prayers.

Contents

Preface

MY HUSBAND, Chris, and I celebrated our fiftieth wedding anniversary on Valentine's Day 1992. When we were married, prayer already was an important part of our lives; but as we faced the complexities of the new marriage relationship and rearing a family, prayer soon became our automatic, spontaneous lifestyle. And for all these years God has answered in many different and sometimes unexpected ways. But He has answered. So through prayer we have had fifty years of indescribable help, specific divine guidance, wonderful comfort, and awesome love—from our Heavenly Father—for our family here on earth.

Many have asked how I know what I should pray for my family members. First, I pray asking God to show me what He wants me to pray. Then I just wait on God to tell me—either as I read His Word, the Bible, or during prayer by His calling to my remembrance the Scripture He wants to be the basis of my prayers for them. Then I write down and date what God said, either in the margin of my Bible or in notes I keep on file. Then I pray. So the whole process is *God*—from Him and then back to Him in prayer. (These two methods are described fully in my book *Lord, Change Me!*)

I have used our favourite family names throughout this book, but for clarity, here are the names of our family members:

Evelyn and Harold (Chris) Christenson.
Daniel and Nancy Thompson with daughters Cynthia (Cindy) and Kathleen (Kathy) Thompson.
Kurt and Margie Christenson with son James.
Spencer (Skip) and Jan with son Brett and daughters Crista and Jennifer (Jenna) Johnson.

You may recognize some of the experiences I recount, since I told about them in former books and in my speaking. It was impossible to draw a complete picture of our family praying without using some of them in this book. Since this book is not fiction, I could not make up illustrations.

The thing that has been hardest in writing this book is that there are thousands of exciting and important prayer answers that could not be included in a book of this size. Deciding what to leave out was my hardest task.

My prayer for you as you read this book is that you will discover not only the awesome power of prayer in your family, as we have in ours, but also the incredible God who answers by reaching down from heaven into your family too. If you have not already done so, I trust that you also will make prayer the spontaneous lifestyle of your family.

CHAPTER ONE

More Than Ever, Our Families Need Prayer

THE CHRISTENSON FAMILY all rejoiced with our daughter Nancy and her husband Dan Thompson when he took a position in 1981 as a financial analyst with a US government agency and went to work in St. Paul for the agency's regional bank. Then in 1985 Dan was transferred to the national office in Washington, DC. By 1987 it was obvious that he had become an extremely valuable worker, for he was honoured as the employee of the year in the agency. And there were prayers of thanksgiving within our family.

Then in May 1988 we got shocking news. When Dan refused to accommodate his boss by falsifying a report to Congress about irregularities in the books of the agency which he had discovered, his job suddenly ended. The word *incompetency* was stamped on his file. This kept him from finding another financial position elsewhere. And even when the Merit Systems Protection Board ruled six months later in Dan's favour, he still could not get another job because his former employer appealed the case—with no time limit forcing a conclusion of the matter.

Our family will never forget the three-and-a-half years that we bombarded heaven with prayers, upholding Dan and Nancy through each emotional and financial crisis.

Later in this book I will tell you about God's amazing answers to these prayers. This I will say now, God is faithful to hear and answer prayer when we earnestly seek Him for our loved ones—whether in relation to a job matter, illness, the birth of a child, the death of a family member, or the salvation of someone we deeply love. And certainly in such problems as rebellion, alcohol and drug addiction, infidelity, and divorce.

Prayer should be the spontaneous lifestyle of every Christian family, especially today because the family as the world has known it for centuries is disintegrating before our eyes. Consider these phone calls and letters that have come to me:

• 'This is Laura calling. My supposedly Christian husband is bringing home pornographic videos and viewing them with our two teenage sons. They contain not only kinky but violent sex, and I have become the brunt of their anti-women abuse.'

• 'My father was brilliant but became a full-fledged alcoholic. His drinking made him so violent our very lives often were endangered. Finally, he was unable to cope with his top management job, settling for caretaker work. Now my married sister blames our mother and for years has not allowed Mother to even see her grandchildren.'

• 'Our daughter rebelled and ran, taking her two children with her. We haven't heard a word from her for two years.'

• 'My husband and I established a Christian home the day we were married. And we brought up our son "in the way he should go," but he did depart from it! He moved out of our house, is on drugs and alcohol, has been in jail several times. Where did we go wrong?'

WHAT IS HAPPENING TO THE FAMILY

Children in many families today have rebelled and blatantly turned their backs on everything they have been taught in their homes. Some have broken all ties with their families and established a new godless lifestyle, frequently involving drugs, illicit sex, and even violence.

It seems popular these days for family members to betray and accuse other members for past inadequacies, leaving confused parents and siblings bleeding in a shattered family unit that seems beyond repair.

For several years now sexual, physical, and emotional child abuse have been escalating at a terrifying rate, and wife battering is alarmingly common, with increasing numbers of cases even of husband abuse reaching the courts.

Marriages broken by infidelity, separation, or divorce are multiplying at an alarming rate, leaving bitter children and an exhausted spouse to hold together what is left. Many one-parent families are struggling just to exist with incomes below the poverty level, bitterly remembering happier days of adequate necessities, good relationships, and a respected family image.

It is not uncommon to find a family member shuddering alone when a devasting tragedy has struck because nobody cared—or even knew. Since current humanism results in individuals looking out for themselves, much of our society and even many of our families have ceased caring for each other.

Financial disaster after financial disaster has left many families' faith in God stretched beyond the breaking point and survival all but impossible.

In our ever-ageing society, many senior citizens feel utterly forsaken by those who should be loving them while increasing numbers of adult children, themselves ageing, are staggering under the heavy burden of round the clock care of a parent.

Still others stand stymied by complex family decisions

that need to be made in the ever-increasing confusion of our modern society.

What we are experiencing in our families today sounds frighteningly like the description of the last days in 2 Timothy:

> For men will be lovers of self, lovers of money, boastful, arrogant, revilers, disobedient to parents, ungrateful, unholy, unloving, irreconcilable, malicious gossips, without self-control, brutal, haters of good, treacherous, reckless, conceited, lovers of pleasure rather than lovers of God; holding a form of godliness, although they have denied its power...always learning but never able to come to the knowledge of the truth (3:2-5, 7).

IS THERE NO HOPE?

Is there hope for today's family? Your family? Yes, there is. Although these symptoms are becoming more and more prevalent in even the best of families, there is an answer. And the answer is prayer. Not just an SOS prayer now and then, but an automatic calling out to God in prayer in every family need. A lifestyle of prayer.

Our daughter-in-love Margie said to me recently, 'I need to learn to pray and not worry. I have a tendency to work things out myself. Think them through and come up with my own answers. But God's Word says it is *prayer* that works.'

The answer to today's disintegrating family is a spontaneous lifestyle of prayer. 'The effectual fervent *prayer* of a righteous man [person] avails much' (James 5:16, italics added).

HUMAN HELP IS NOT ENOUGH

Won't counselling and friendly advice help just as much? Might not the results be even better if we seek human professional help? No, because prayer invites not just *any person* but *a certain Person* into the family situation—a supernatural, divine Being to intervene, assist, direct, instruct, rebuke, solve the problems—and heal.

There are many helpful resources available in books, seminars, and counselling today (some also are very bad), and the good ones certainly can help in the important step of identifying the family problems. And, if following biblical principles, they can lead through many of the steps of recovery and reconciliation. However, secular intellectual human help is not sufficient by itself. *Only God has the power to reach down and complete the final healing step that mends the broken family members.*

The 'Age of Enlightenment' as a cure-all is fizzling because as knowledge has increased, evil has escalated. Social reform through communism is dead. Materialism in our families has failed to bring sought-after peace. These things didn't work. Why? Because there is another dimension in us that needs curing—the spirit. 'The fool has said in his heart, "There is no God" ' (Ps. 14:1).

Also, prayer relies on the God who can run a family without ever making a mistake. It invites the God who knows the outcome from the beginning of every situation to be in control of the family.

Why should prayer be the automatic, spontaneous life-style in our families? *Because from everyday hassles to devastating family catastrophies, prayer enlists the help of the omnipotent, omnipresent God of the universe who is willing and even eager to release His divine power into the lives of our family members.* Only God, not humans, can do that!

> Be anxious for nothing, but in everything by prayer and supplication with thanksgiving let your requests be made *to God* (Phil. 4:6, italics added).

Mary George, a tiny Philadelphia woman known to long-time friends as 'the girl of prayer,' tells of a time when she and her six sisters and a brother were facing eviction, since the house's owner wanted to convert their home into a block of flats . Their parents had died, and the house they lived in was in dire need of repair—a leaking roof, a broken water heater, and ceilings about to fall.

The condition of the old house prompted a friend, Susie Bahner, to write a song based on the tune 'This World Is Not My Home'. the first verse and chorus going like this:

> This house is not our home,
> We're just existing here;
> The ceiling's falling down,
> And Esther's full of fear.
> The kitchen's full of things
> That run around at night,
> And the dining room ceiling is really a sight.
> O Lord, You know that we must all be out;
> On January 24th we'll wander all about.
> We only need a dime to open our front door,
> And we don't feel at home in this house any more!

Yet the landlord had given the family notice that they had to move, and finding a house large enough for the family of eight, and one they could afford, wasn't easy. They prayed and prayed about a place to go, both individually and as a family.

Inquiring about a house a block away, they were informed a potential buyer was settling the next day. But the owner phoned later to tell that family of children that the buyer had backed out of the sale, and she would rent the house to them.

Mary recalls, 'The next day we signed the lease, and word got around the neighbourhood how God had taken care of the Georges. Immediately, we had neighbours and friends volunteering to help us clean and do repairs, and make the house livable. The next few days, up and down the streets, people were heard saying, *"Have you heard how God took care of the Georges?"* ' Family prayer!

PRAYER INVOLVES GOD

How can a simple thing like prayer do such a monumental job in our families? When our children have rebelled and broken the family ties, prayer calls on God who always can and will reach out to them no matter where they are scattered around the earth. He will intervene in their lives no matter what they are doing. This is the God who can muster ten thousand angels to protect them in the most dangerous situations and rescue them in all crises—*if we pray*.

When there has been a betrayal or hurtful accusation by another family member, how wonderful it is to be able to turn to our God. The God who is absolute truth in the midst of deceit, denial, and duplicity of family members to one another. The God who never has memory lapses like us humans or remembers incorrectly. The God who is absolutely impartial, who is always 100 percent fair, and never sees through prejudiced eyes. Our God who never is spiteful or petty as we family members sometimes are but always does all things for all the family members' good. Yes, He even helps us forgive when we can't and helps us love when we are unable or unwilling. Prayer breaks down barriers we have built for days or even years. The God of our prayers melts stony, stubborn hearts.

In the midst of abuse and mistreatment that some family members are powerless to avoid, the suffering ones can cry out to their God who reaches out and holds us close to His loving breast. And in the years of recovering from past abuses, it is *only* our God who can bring that complete and permanent healing so desperately needed for full emotional, physical, mental, and spiritual restoration.

In broken marriages, prayer invites the Heavenly Father into the headship role of the remaining family: a family head who loves unconditionally and never breaks a promise.

In our loneliness, prayer will bring the God who never forsakes or betrays any family member. For the ageing parent, prayer calls on a Person who never slumbers or sleeps, who never ignores, or who never is too busy to give His undivided attention—all of the time.

In financial disasters, we can trust the God who will provide, sometimes in miraculous ways, for our needs.

Prayer may or may not remove the difficult circumstances, but it will give grace and courage to face them. Prayer doesn't necessarily remove every storm, but it definitely will calm the family in the storm.

Prayer guarantees a Companion in our homes when tragedy strikes. A Friend who will gently hold our hand or hold us close to Himself in His everlasting arms. Or even pick us up and carry us when we cannot go on. The Great Physician. The One who comforts in all our deepest family sorrows.

In our family's confusion when we have lost our way, prayer introduces an omniscient, all-knowing God who gives wisdom and peace. Who always knows which decision we should make. Who knows the 'what ifs' of our intended course of action. Knows what disasters would happen if our human plans—not His—were followed.

Prayer gives the family the privilege of depending on an all-knowing, all-powerful and all-caring Person—who can be with every family member every minute—everywhere. God!

FIRST PRAYER IN THE BIBLE IS ABOUT FAMILIES

The first time the word *prayer* was used in the Bible was in a family situation (see Gen. 20:7 and 17). After Abraham deceived Abimelech into thinking Sarah was his sister, to keep from being killed, God revealed the truth to Abimelech in a dream telling him to restore Sarah and then Abraham would *pray* for him. The Lord had closed fast all the wombs of the household of Abimelech because of his taking Sarah; and then 'Abraham *prayed* to God; and God healed Abimelech and his wife and his maids so that they bore children' (Gen. 20:17, italics added). And prayer has been a critical part of biblical family life ever since.

SO WHY DO SO FEW PRAY?

While being interviewed by a Christian counsellor in California, I was asked a very profound question. 'Evelyn, since all Christians know that there is power and guidance in prayer, why is it so few of them really pray diligently and fervently?'

'There are many reasons,' I answered, 'but one of the main ones is pride. It is hard to admit we need help or that our way of doing it may not be right. In fact,' I continued, 'deep down in their hearts many Christians are saying *"I can do it myself, God!"* '

Also many people glibly say, 'All's well that ends well.' But this is just wishful thinking and not true if they haven't included God in their human handling of circumstances and events.

How foolish it is to depend on our inadequate, limited, and biased opinions and wisdom—when we don't pray.

How foolish to deprive our families of all that fantastic good—when we don't pray.

How surprising that Christian families grope and stumble and sometimes break up—because they have not bothered to call for God's help.

The Bible clearly says one of the main reasons we don't have solutions to our family problems is that we have not asked God for them. We have not prayed. 'You have not because you ask not' (James 4:2).

But when we do pray, God releases His divine power into the life of our family members for whom we are praying.

Our prayer groups in our 'What Happens When Women Pray' church joined a devastated mother and father praying persistently for their son. He had left his family's Christian lifestyle for one of organized crime. It took years of their praying—and ours. But prayer did work. Today he is the father of a fine family and one of the leaders of a good church.

As I was typing this page, a member of that church called to say hello. 'I want to tell you that prayer really does work, Evelyn,' said the caller, a father. 'One of our sons was in the lowest quarter of his high school class and almost failed his first year of college. And now he is a dedicated maths teacher in our very fine local Christian high school. And prayer did it!'

Another family from that church had a daughter who was breaking their hearts. She rebelled against the Christian leadership lifestyle of her parents and many times refused to go to high school. She ended up running from the family, on drugs, and in a godless lifestyle. But our prayer groups joined her praying parents also—praying almost daily. And now she and her husband have a successful ministry in Hollywood reaching those in the movie industry for Jesus.

OUR FAMILY'S LIFESTYLE

God has literally run my family through prayer. Our multiple family problems have kept us on our faces before God. Many, many times our dependence on Him has been our means of survival. But God has been in control of our family decisions, relationships, joys, and trials. In these fifty years of marriage, our family has had a spontaneous lifestyle of prayer.

Since becoming a mother and a grandmother, I know what the Bible means by the admonition 'Pray without ceasing' (1 Thes. 5:17).

It is not just the bedtime praying of my husband and me which always includes each of the family members. Not just my daily morning devotions when I always intercede fervently for our family members. It is not just the formal times we pray together for each other, or the spontaneous quick prayers when a need suddenly arises. No, family prayer is the lifestyle of our family—independently and with each other.

Also, each of my family members does not get the same amount or intensity of prayer each day. Family prayers are not a formal listing of each member in a prayer diary to be dutifully or even perfunctorily prayed through. *No, the time spent on each is directly in proportion to that individual's need that day.*

Prayer is sweeping my grandchildren into my arms when they are afraid—thanking God with them for His protection. It is pacing with an infant granddaughter with colic, breathing a continuous prayer for relief. It is including God's comfort along with the bandage on a skinned knee. It is asking for God's healing as a hand is laid comfortingly on a sick tummy or fevered forehead—or for a husband during surgery. It is clinging in faith to God while pacing the floor with the unwashed grandchild while the surgeons race to save a daughter's life. It is agonizing through sleepless nights for a wayward child.

Prayer in our family isn't something we do occasionally; it is a way of life. *A life lived moment by moment with the most important member of our family—the God of the universe.*

And God is longing to be the most important member of your family too.

PRAYER IS NOT A COP-OUT

People frequently tell me they believe we often use prayer instead of handling a problem ourselves. They believe prayer is used by people who aren't smart enough or brave enough to run their own lives. That is not true. Prayer is just one step in the process of identifying the problem and then getting the instructions as to how to handle it from God. But it is by far the most important step.

Prayer is including God in our course of action instead of bungling through with our incomplete, biased, and sometimes inaccurate human thinking. Only by seeking God—in prayer—do we have His divine wisdom and input into the family situation.

Of course, after praying, we 'put feet to our prayers' and obey what God has directed us to say or do or be. Prayer is not *in place of* action, it is just getting the wisdom and power *for* that action.

PRAYER ACKNOWLEDGES GOD AS DIRECTOR OF OUR FAMILIES

I have had special days that I waited in prayer on God for particular Scripture verses of guidance. For example, when Chris and I were pastoring in Rockford, God would give me the same New Year's Scripture year after year—Proverbs 3:5-6:

> Trust in the Lord with all your heart, and lean not on your own understanding. In all thy ways acknowledge Him, and He will direct your paths (AV).

At first I was thrilled at knowing He wanted to direct me and my family the next year, and enthusiastically practiced letting Him do it. But as the years passed, and He kept giving me the same Scripture, I became impatient. Was God in a rut? Or had He run out of new ideas for me?

But now I realize that this was a very deliberate repetition, reinforcing the greatest lesson of my life: *If I DON'T lean on my own understanding, and if I DO trust in Him, and if in all my ways I DO acknowledge Him—then, and only then, will God direct my own and our family's paths.*

And how do I acknowledge Him? By running my life by prayer. Depending on Him instead of myself.

I have found this guidance as precise, tangible, definite, and accurate as the star of Bethlehem leading the magi to the Christ Child (Matt. 2:9). When they left Herod, the star appeared again very clearly to them and directed them to the Child. So also with me. The same words apply to my life. *He will direct our paths*—through prayer.

WHEN WE DON'T KNOW HOW TO PRAY

However, there are those times when we don't know how to pray for our families. But God has provided me the solution to that problem too. The Father gave us the Holy Spirit to live in us—who prays to Him whatever is the Father's will—when we don't know how to pray.

And in the same way the Spirit also helps our weakness; for we do not know how to pray as we should, but the Spirit Himself intercedes for us with groanings too deep for words; and He who searches the hearts knows what the mind of the Spirit is, because He intercedes for the saints according to the will of God (Rom. 8:26-27).

Our daughter Nancy called recently saying that her five-year-old Kathy was going through a stage—arrogant, bossy, and aggressive. Remembering her older sister's similar attitude and the spiritual warfare prayer against Satan that changed her completely, I started to pray the same for Kathy. But somehow it wasn't right.

Finally, kneeling in the living room, I prayed, 'O Holy Spirit, I don't know how or what to pray for Kathy. Please take my "not knowing how to pray as I ought" to the Father according to His will.'

What a relief! The pressure to figure out just what to pray left me. I knew God knew exactly what Kathy needed—and the Holy Spirit would take my inadequate prayer to the Father exactly according to the Father's will.

Talking to Nancy the next day, I asked about Kathy. A little surprised, she said, 'Oh, she seems so much better.' I thought, *I wonder* how *God answered my prayer of not knowing what to pray? Well, I don't need to know as long as God knows— and answers!*

One of the greatest helps to me in my family praying throughout the years has been the burden the Holy Spirit has lifted from me when I don't know how to pray in family situations.

NO PRAYER IN THE GARDEN OF EDEN

God's original plan for Planet Earth did not include prayer. When God put the first family in the Garden of Eden, there was no family prayer. Why? Because Adam and Eve didn't need it. In the first home established on earth, there was perfect face-to-face communication with God. 'They heard the sound of the Lord God walking in the garden in the cool of the day' (Gen. 3:8).

And God carried on direct conversations with them, asking them questions and getting answers from Adam and Eve. They were open, personal friends.

So, why do we need prayer now? Because of *sin*. When Satan brought sin to earth through our first parents, God drove Adam and Eve out of their perfect environment and relationship with Him. Sin destroyed humans' perfect two-way communication with God.

But God's communicating with people did not cease; it just changed form. *He then instituted prayer.* In Genesis 4:26 we read this about Adam and Eve's son Seth: 'Then men began to call upon the name of the Lord.'

And we can see prayer developing throughout the Bible until today when we have communication with the Father restored by Jesus on the cross. Adam and Eve's perfect communion with the Father is available to us, His children. Sweet, unbroken communion has been restored by the shed blood of Jesus Christ—for our families.

> Having therefore, brethren, boldness to enter into the holiest by the blood of Jesus (Heb. 10:19, av).

Once we have availed ourselves of that cleansing and redeeming blood of Jesus in salvation, we are eligible for this ideal relationship of unbroken communication with God.

PRAYER RECOVERS FOR US WHAT WE LOST THROUGH SIN

God provided prayer as the means of recovering those things which humans lost when sin took over Planet Earth.

First, in the Old Testament prayer restored people's communication with God, and prayer in the name of Jesus restored human beings' perfect communion with God. Jesus said:

> Until now you have asked for nothing in My name; ask and you will receive, that your joy may be made full (John 16:24).

A second thing restored by God is *boldness* in people's coming to Him in prayer. Are you afraid to approach the holy God of heaven with your family needs? Afraid He won't want to be bothered by your problems? Afraid He won't answer? Adam and Eve had no inhibitions about talking to God—until they hid themselves from Him because of their sinning. But God provided forgiveness for our sins through Jesus—and confidence to come to His throne.

> 'Let us therefore [because of our High Priest Jesus] draw near with confidence [boldness] to the throne of grace' (Heb. 4:16).

Amazingly, a third thing lost to humans through Adam and Eve's sin—and was restored through prayer—is *dominion*.

When God created the first parents and placed them in the Garden, He said to them, 'Be fruitful and multiply, and fill the earth and subdue it; and rule over...every living thing that moves on the earth' (Gen. 1:28). But at their sinning, the whole world fell into Satan's domain. The human race had forfeited its right to rule the earth. And 1 John 5:19 is still true today, 'The whole world lies in the power of the evil one.'

After the Fall God chose a new way to let His children help Him rule the earth. It is through *intercessory prayer*. This, of course, is not the direct dominion it would have been had humans not sinned; but, nevertheless, prayer does assist God today in ruling the earth.

Andrew Murray, my favourite devotional author, wrote, 'Most churches don't know that God rules the world by the prayers of His saints.' And that includes our families—here in the world.

We must never forget that God is sovereign; but all through the Bible we find promises that when we pray, He will act. In prayer, we move the hand that moves everything in the world—including our families.

> Ask, and it shall be given to you; seek, and you shall find; knock, and it shall be opened to you. For everyone who asks receives, and he who seeks finds, and to him who knocks it shall be opened (Matt. 7:7-8).

When through rebellion or separation we feel we have lost all influence or control over the wayward family members, we can pray up to God, who in turn reaches down to them. And He brings His holy influence to bear upon them. There may be nothing we can do directly because of their having broken our relationship, but God can—and will.

PRAYER WORKS!
Since Chris and I celebrated our fiftieth wedding anniversary, I no longer have to say about family prayer, 'I think' or 'I hope' it will work. No, after our family has prayed for half a century, I now *know* that prayer really does work.

When I was young, I had to take so much on faith. But not any more! Frequently, it takes years for us to see the final answer to prayers prayed with and for the family. And some we don't recognize as answers. Some we even forget we prayed for. And some we won't know the answers until we get to heaven. But, nevertheless, God *is* answering!

One of my most exciting answers to prayer in our family came when our son Kurt applied for the doctoral programme in physics at the University of Illinois. After going to lectures all day, he had to take three-hour entrance exams on two consecutive nights. And I had promised to pray while he took them. I spent those two three-hour evenings staying only in prayer, alternately moving from pleading on my knees to seeking direction from God in the Bible. From struggling long over releasing my son to God's will, not mine—to the piano to worship God for being in control of our family—to praising Him in advance for however He was going to answer.

I had gone to bed exhausted—and prayer *is* hard work—after I knew Kurt had finally finished. But my heart leaped with joy as I sleepily answered the phone and heard the telephone operator struggling to say, 'Will you accept a collect call from physics doctoral candidate Kurt Karl Christenson?' His way of announcing that God had answered my prayers! He had passed.

A few years later my daughter-in-love Margie wrote me a letter soon after her marriage to Kurt. 'I appreciate the personal example you have set for your family as a praying mother, and I guess this is really what inspired me the most and keeps on inspiring me. I've thought a lot about your praying for three hours just for Kurt. A person's life tells the best story.'

Then there also are those squeezes of my hand with a grateful quick smile and, 'Thanks, Mom, for praying.'

Or the 'Call-the-prayer-chain-quick,-Mother' phone call when calamity strikes them or a friend.

Or the endless sighing, 'Please pray *again*, Mom,' when a hurting problem still hasn't been solved.

Our daughter Jan just told me that she heard their six-year-old Crista vomiting in the bathroom and she dashed in to help her. Our Jan said as she pulled Crista's hair back out of her face and held on to her, Crista gasped, 'Pray for me, Mom. Pray!'

In fifty years of marriage, Chris and I have left many imprints on our family, some good and some not so good. But the greatest legacy we ever could leave our children and their children is their seeing and knowing the importance and power of family prayer.

Prayer should be, and can be, the spontaneous lifestyle of every Christian family.

CHAPTER TWO

Crisscross Praying

WHEN A BRIDE AND GROOM establish a new Christian home, they start to weave the fabric of which their home will be made. Of all the things they begin to weave into their newly formed family, prayer is by far the most important. Love, fidelity, mutual respect, support, and serving each other are all vitally necessary—but prayers are the threads that weave the fabric which God uses to hold a family together.

Fifty years ago when Chris and I were married, we founded our family on prayer. Through the years we have experienced disasters, deaths, rebellions, and going to war. But the fabric of undergirding prayer we wove has stood the test of time; God Himself has been crisscrossed through the fabric of our home.

When a new couple starts building their home on God through prayer, they begin crisscrossing their individual and mutual strands of prayer. These form the warp (the threads extending lengthwise in a loom) and the weft (the threads that cross the warp) of a potentially impenetrable woven foundation for their home and marriage.

CHILDREN CAN ALSO BE PRAY-ERS

Through the years the family praying expands. As the children mature, they also can become pray-ers, not just the objects of prayer. The threads of prayer then come from several directions for each other. From the time our first child, Jan, started kindergarten to when our last child, Kurt, graduated from high school, Chris or I prayed with them at the door, sending each off with the Lord protecting and guiding. It was so reassuring to our children and us that they weren't going out to meet the world alone but going out under God's care. It gave confidence, quelling the fear of what they might encounter. Yet it was always Chris and I—the parents—praying for our children.

However, one day a new kind of prayer emerged in that 'front door praying.' I had just finished praying for our grade-schooler Nancy, when I said, 'Honey, Mother has a problem today. Would you please pray for me too?' And joy filled that front hall as my child took her little, immature but oh-so-sincere thread of prayer and wove it haltingly into the fabric we called family prayer.

I have brought our children up absolutely knowing that I need them to pray for me—because I tell them. Frequently, what they pray is the Scripture verses God gives them for me. While writing one of my books, I struggled to have enough courage to say the things God clearly was telling me to say. Our daughter Jan wrote me a note with her prayer for me from Ephesians 6:19-20:

> Pray for me also, that whenever I open my mouth, words may be given me so that I will fearlessly make known the mystery of the Gospel. Pray that I may declare it fearlessly, as I should.
> Love, Janny

I taped her note to my word processor, rereading it whenever my boldness started to falter—and never once writing less than what God told me to. God answering my daughter's prayers for me! And that note is taped up by my computer to this day.

Children's prayers are heard by the Heavenly Father. The chairman of our Metropolitan Prayer Chain told me that all her children received Jesus before she and her husband did. 'It was my children's prayers for our salvation,' she told me, 'that brought their father and me to Jesus.'

Crisscrossing prayers has spilled over into our extended family. For example, our doctor son-in-law Skip Johnson (I call him my 'son-in-love') was teaching a Sunday School class, and Jan and their two little daughters, Jenna and Crista, had gone alone to pray for him while he taught. However, the next week, the older daughter, Jenna, was in the class listening to him. She asked her dad if she could be excused to go to the toilet, but later told him her reason was to go there to pray alone for him while he was teaching.

As our three children's praying for us parents grew, an exciting and powerful dimension of family prayer developed. Crisscrossing with our children emerged. And the fabric of our family praying solidified day after day, year after year, as we all wove our threads of prayer every which way—sometimes with bursts of enthusiasm, sometimes with urgency, and even sometimes with apathy. But little by little the weaving progressed.

PRAYER—HOPE FOR ONE-PARENT FAMILIES

Today many children in the world are from single-parent families. Is there any hope for them? Does it take the traditional family of a father, mother, and children to have an effective prayer life? Not so. I have seen an unusually strong prayer base develop in many single-parent families as they struggled to survive financially and emotionally. When their forced dependence on each other turns also to a dependence on God in prayer, an incredibly strong fabric of support from the omnipotent God of the universe weaves through their family relationship.

I have received many phone calls and letters about a straying husband and father—and occasionally about a straying mother. In each instance a traditional family has been shattered. And I am astounded at how many mothers say, 'My children and I are praying for our daddy every day. We're praying that he will turn back to God, and then that he will come home to us.' Frequently, they expect my praying to bring him home immediately, so I gently remind them that God gave everybody, including their daddy, a free will. A straying father still can, and frequently does, choose to live in his sin; and it is only prayer that can reach him. So I join in praying that God will reach out, convict him of his sin, and call him back first to Himself and then to his family. This is a situation in which the children of a fragmented family can join Mother (or Father) with their strands of prayer—for a reunited family.

WHEN THERE'S ONLY ONE PRAY-ER

Even in many traditional Christian families, all too often there is only one member—a wife, husband, mother or father, or sometimes a mature child—who intercedes for other family members, perhaps for a family member who has strayed from godly teaching and is living in sin. The lone pray-er may pray fervently, month in and month out or even year after year, weeping and agonizing before God.

In my many years of ministry, the vast majority of phone calls and letters I receive have come from faithful Christian wives and mothers asking prayer for their husbands and children. Not long ago a mother teaching her six children at home came to one of my prayer training sessions to get a new lease on her praying. Her husband was in prison, and the burden she carried all alone was almost more than she could bear.

Yes, if only one parent or another pray-er believes in the power of prayer, there is hope for that family despite a pulling in opposite directions of priorities, lifestyles, and goals. There may be open opposition and even ridicule about depending on God through prayer. But it can work even if there is only one pray-er. It worked in my own home as I was growing up. My mother was the one who prayed, never giving up, teaching us the Scriptures and living her Jesus before us.

In the case of a lone believing parent, the New Testament bears out that it is definitely possible to bring up a child the scriptural way he should go. Timothy was the 'son of a Jewish women and believed, but his father was a Greek' unbeliever (Acts 16:1). The Apostle Paul attests in 2 Timothy 1:5 to the fact that his young co-worker, Timothy, became a Christian through his mother and believing grandmother and mentions it further in chapter 3 (vv. 14-15):

> You, however, continue in the things you have learned and become convinced of, knowing from whom you have learned them; and that from childhood you have known the sacred writings which are able to give you the wisdom that leads to salvation through faith which is in Christ Jesus.

Again, it may seem so lonely and sometimes almost futile, but God does hear and answer those prayers woven all alone by just one pray-er through days and even years.

> The effectual fervent prayer of a righteous person avails much (James 5:15, av).

PRAYING GRANDPARENTS

As indicated earlier, Grandmother Lois evidently played an important role in the spiritual nurturing of Timothy. The praying of the grandmothers (now great-grandmothers) in our own immediate family have produced changed lives and an ongoing stability and security in our extended family as well.

Our Grandma Chris started praying for every one of her

family members more than seventy years ago upon receiving Jesus as her Saviour and Lord when she was twenty-one. As the years passed, she prayed while working at the kitchen sink, a Bible promise stuck up in the window, or as she knelt in her bedroom. Now at ninety-one, too feeble to kneel, Grandma Chris still continues to pray in her rocking chair, each day reminding God of the needs of each child, grandchild, and great-grandchild. Though helpless to do anything personally when family needs arise, she knows who can help—her Heavenly Father.

Because of the myriad of answers to prayer through all those seventy plus years, she has immovable faith in God's prayer promise. So unshakable was her faith in God's answering prayers that when her husband, Rudolph, died, leaving her with two children, aged nine and twelve, to bring up alone, day in and day out her anchor in prayer was: 'As thy days, so shall thy strength be' (Deut. 33:25, AV). When there wasn't food for the table or coal for the old furnace, there was always her never-failing God answering her prayers.

My own mother had an especially hard life when I was a child. My parents ran a greenhouse and florist's shop. Mother had serious asthma, but would always take her turn to go down two flights of stairs in the middle of the winter nights to stoke the big furnace with coal. Even when pregnant, she never stopped carrying big loads of plants, soil, and pots. But prayer sustained her.

When things got really difficult, we knew where to find our mother—in the middle of the calla lily bed, with the almost ethereal purity of those huge waxy white flowers surrounding her, as she stood serenely praying. And pray she did, until God called her home five years ago. She prayed according to 1 Thessalonians 5:17—'without ceasing'. She prayed while she worked, while she made as many as a hundred quilts a year for missionaries, while she rolled thousands of bandages for medical missionaries until the wee hours of the morning. The hours of intercessory prayer she managed to carve out of her very busy schedule were basically for her offspring. She prayed us through difficult births, deaths, times of family conflict, financial disasters, educations, career changes—anything else that came up. And we all knew it. So we would call our mother immediately when our world started to fall apart—because we knew that her hotline to heaven never shut down.

BLESSED ARE THOSE WITH 'PRAYER ROOTS'

Many newly married couples bring into their marriage a strong prayer network from one or both of their families. However, as they leave their father and mother and become one flesh (see Gen. 2:24), they do start weaving a new fabric of prayer for their own emerging family. Before a new family unit is organized, godly parents may have spent many, many years praying for that future family unit. All of this prayer is used by God to help weave the new family's prayer fabric.

After our marriage Chris and I as a new family unit had that kind of support. We had three praying parents, all of whom prayed for years that each of us would marry the person God intended for us. Chris' father was a 'godly spiritual giant'. With my new husband fighting in World War II as a bomber pilot, I spent many nights in the home of Chris' parents. But I never could get up earlier than Grandpa Chris. Every morning I would find him kneeling in prayer—huddled up on a cold Michigan winter morning absorbing the little heat that his newly laid coal fire was sending his way. His powerful prayer life, along with Grandma Chris', gave our marriage a spiritual send-off with God.

With such a heritage, we also prayed for years and years for the mates God knew were right for each of our children. And God over the years answered!

THE MULTIPLYING FAMILY

When the children eventually take a spouse of their own, they not only form their own new family, but their continued prayers for the other members of their families strengthen the original family unit. And, of course, when other family members pray for them, their new undergirding fabric of prayer is continuously strengthened by the other prayer threads weaving in and out. This is not just being prayed for by the original parents, but results in crisscrossing prayers flowing in all directions. The seemingly haphazard pattern is actually producing an amazingly strong network of woven support of prayer for the multiplying family.

So, through the years, an actual *network* of prayer develops with as many starting points as there are family members, weaving in as many directions as those members choose to pray faithfully for their siblings, parents, grandparents, close and distant relatives.

However, that crisscrossing is not just an inert, lifeless network. No, it is everchanging in intensity and frequency as family members' needs come and go. And changing personal relationships within the family determine the quality and quantity of the praying. This, of course, changes the strength of the prayer network—for better or for worse.

The first time my daughter-in-love Margie heard me speak, she and our son, Kurt, were newlyweds. I found myself carefully guarding my illustrations of answered prayer so as not to intimidate her or overwhelm her with what she might consider a 'preachy' mother-in-law. But a note passed up to me during the seminar quelled my fears and thrilled my heart:

> I love you so much. We are enjoying being here, praying together—and with God. Keep preaching it! We're praying for you in the back pew! Love, Margie and Kurt

Crisscrossing prayers produce strong family ties—not

just based on tradition, fun, and family celebrations—but on a deepening *caring* as the prayers continue to weave a stronger and stronger family network.

When a dog almost bit off the nose of one of our grand-daughters, God performed an absolute miracle; there were virtually no scars in answer to desperate family praying. After my husband, Chris, underwent cancer surgery, he said, because of so many prayers, he felt as if his body were on air, not even touching the hospital bed. Our family prayer network has undergirded one family member during a period of deep financial distress. Entrance exams to colleges and postgraduate studies have been prayed through by the family. There was a prayer vigil during labour and delivery of all the new babies in the family. The list is endless. But in each need, the dimension producing the results was *family prayers*.

When our family lived in Rockford, Illinois, in the 1960s, a tornado passed through while I was alone with our three children. Lightning hit the outside electric wires and travelled through two rooms to a socket in the living room. En route to another state, Chris kept track of the storm's path by radio; and, as soon as it had passed our home, he called long distance. Stunned, I picked up the phone and answered that, yes, we all were safe, but the house had just been hit by lightning.

The city firemen left, though they still felt heat in the walls where the lightning had travelled—and still smelled smoke. I listened in awe as they informed me not to go to sleep but to keep watching for a possible outbreak of fire. The excitement of the big hook-and-ladder fire truck, the curious gawking neighbours, and the fear of fire still some-where in our walls had the children and me fearful and on edge. But then the children and I all knelt by Nancy's bed to pray before they tried to settle down. And it was Kurt, still in primary school, who calmed us all with his immedi-ate prayer, 'Dear God, thank You that we don't need to be afraid.' We continued to keep alert, but the danger passed.

Family crises, large and small, have sent our whole family to our knees through all these years. A book could be written on all the times God has intervened, rescued, and performed miracles—*when we prayed for each other*.

THE EXTENDED FAMILY

Our family praying extends an incredibly long way out, because what we consider family includes aunts, uncles, cousins, nieces, nephews, and even 'second' and 'third' relatives. Although we usually only pray for these when deeper needs arise, it is a joy to stretch our threads of family prayer beyond our immediate family unit to those even remotely connected to us.

When my nephew Bud was murdered some years ago, much of our praying was for his only son, Budde—left fatherless and very bitter toward the police for doing such a seemingly incomplete investigation of the crime. Our extended family fervently and persistently prayed for God to take over in the boy's life. And we especially asked God to bring a good Christian man to help fill the void left by Budde's father's death. Just two years later we were thrilled at how he had lost most of his bitterness toward the police and was amazingly well adjusted. God had brought the right man, a man who took him through the Eagle Scout badge in Boy Scouts and guided him as he attended a good church. *Extended family praying!*

Our grandniece Kirsten was finishing some necessary course work for college and stayed temporarily with us when our daughter Nancy called from Virginia. Distraught, Nancy asked us to pray immediately for a Christian school for Cindy, since the one in which she was registered had been closed for a minor infraction of a rule—and she had until only 2 o'clock that day to enroll Cindy somewhere else.

A few quick phone calls revealed that my prayer chain members had all scattered for the holiday weekend, nor was I able to contact any other family members. So Chris, niece

Kirsten, and I bowed our heads at the kitchen table, calling upon God to intervene. Then Kirsten prayed with profound insight, 'Dear God, put Cindy where it will be best for her. You know how devastating the first day of a new school can be. Protect her emotionally in her fear and in the horror of not being included in a school her first day away from nursery school at her own church.'

Shortly after 2 p.m. Nancy called, spilling out the details of how she had found an academically sound, prestigious school. But, without Nancy knowing it, that school had a bus pickup at Cindy's old nursery school, where her sister, Kathy, would be going every day—and where many of Cindy's friends would be boarding the school bus with her. Cindy could continue with her usual after-school care the days both parents had to be working—and with both her friends and sister, Kathy! How we needed that prayer from an extended family member—Kirsten.

RIPS AND HOLES

In all families there are times when a few individuals or even all family members squabble and have misunderstandings, ripping holes in the undergirding fabric which has been woven by prayer. Some holes are easily patched and hardly affect the strength of the network at all; in some cases squabbles rip huge gaps in the prayer fabric, causing a serious disruption in the flow of family prayers or even a ceasing of praying altogether.

But again, it is the threads of prayer that can mend the snags and gaping holes in family relationships. During the Depression of the 1930s, I used to watch my mother darn socks. She would take one strand of darning thread and painstakingly weave it back and forth until what was a hole was stronger than the original sock. That is how prayer mends a family's rips and holes.

Through the years, I have prayed many, many times in the words of the Apostle Paul's desire for the family of believers in Corinth when there were quarrels among them:

> Now I exhort you, brethren, by the name of our Lord Jesus
> Christ that you all agree, and there be no divisions among
> you, but you be made complete in the same mind and in the
> same judgment (1 Cor. 1:10).

So it is with just one, or perhaps a few, family members
taking their threads of prayer and patiently, often
painstakingly, weaving to mend the family fabric. Sometimes the weaving accomplishes its purpose quickly, but
sometimes it takes faithful weaving for years before the rift
is mended. Much mending prayer is done in weeping and
even agonizing of spirit. But, stitch by stitch, God lifts His
holy hand and pulls those threads of prayer in place, supernaturally mending those hurtful holes.

WHEN OTHERS PRAY FOR MY FAMILY

I haven't tried to pray for my family by myself since 1964,
but instead have enlisted help in praying for our immediate
family. For twenty-eight years there have been organized
prayer groups, telephone prayer chains, and individual
non-family members praying for our family. We feel
unusually blessed of the Lord to have had this rare privilege.

From 1964 through 1967, Signe Swan, Lorna Johnson,
and I met every week to pray for our church—and also for
our families' needs. Then in 1968 during our 'What Happens When Women Pray' experiment, we organized the
first telephone prayer chains. And until we left that Rockford pastorate three years later, according to our carefully
kept records, our family needs were voiced to God an aver-
age of four times a week on those telephone prayer chains.
That prayer experimentation had a great influence on our
whole church. When the most difficult disaster came to our
parsonage family, the whole church undergirded us in
prayer. On one unbelievably hard day, the deacon board
divided up the day and kept up unbroken prayer for us for
twenty-four hours!

Immediately following our move to St. Paul, I organized

a group of praying women into a monthly ministry support-
ing prayer group and a telephone prayer chain, which kept
daily prayer for me and my family going up to our Heavenly
Father for fifteen years. Then in 1973 we incorporated our
United Prayer Ministries, and until this day my telephone
prayer chairman calls me by 6:20 a.m. three times every
week. This is my ministry prayer chain involving some
thirty women, but always included are the prayer needs for
my family. I share our needs—and they all pray! Then at
my monthly board meetings we pray at least half of the
time, and all deep needs of my family are included with
other families' needs.

Then I have a host of people around the world who have
picked up family needs from my illustrations in seminars,
prayer warriors who not only pray for us but enlist their
prayer groups and chains to do so also. I am continually
surprised as notes and phone calls tell me God has laid on
their hearts to pray for my family. Frequently, it has been
even beyond what I understood the problem or need to
be—but God knew and told them to pray. This is an
overwhelming privilege which I don't deserve but for which
I am so grateful!

So this too has become a way of life for our family. It is
second nature for our children to 'call the prayer chain'.
The last time I was in India, Grandma Chris went into a
coma, not expected to live. Our daughter Jan immediately
called the prayer chain—and they joined family members
in praying God's will and God's timing. Then, getting word
to me in Calcutta, my national chairman there alerted all
the city chairmen where I was to speak of the possibility of
my having to go home. And immediately they all mustered
their pray-ers all over India. To the astonishment of the
doctors, Grandma Chris rallied—and I could continue my
prayer tour of India laying the groundwork for the first
national women's movement ever in that country—a prayer organization.

MY SPECIAL PLACE OF PRAYER

My old green prayer chair has been replaced. When we moved into our present house, there was not room for that big old green chair which had been my place of prayer— my 'prayer closet'—for so many years. Now I have what I call my 'prayer pouf'.

Since my ministry was prayed into existence around my vice president's prayer pouf over twenty years ago, I had wanted one in my house. A few years ago we ordered an oversized tufted footstool to serve as my prayer pouf. My heart leaped with ecstatic joy, and tears sprang up in my eyes as I checked it in the warehouse before it was delivered.

After my excited granddaughters Jenna and Crista watched the big truck deliver it, I suggested that the three of us practice so we could teach their mummy and daddy how to pray there. But six-year-old Jenna replied, 'I don't have to; I already did!'

The first time we knelt around it to pray, it was an invitation to three-year-old Crista to crawl up on Grandma's back and play piggyback. Sometime afterwards, several family members were casually discussing the name I had given that new piece of furniture—the 'prayer pouf'. Suddenly Crista decided we should pray right then. 'I know how to kneel,' she announced, and she promptly knelt to show us. When her invitation of 'let's pray' came so uninhibited out of her mouth, we all eagerly knelt and called the rest of the family to join us. When Crista's daddy, Skip, suggested, 'Why don't you pray first, Crista?' there was a short pause, and we could almost hear her wondering, *What do I do now?* But then she bravely launched into her prayer about the thing uppermost in her mind right then, 'Thank You, Lord, for the wonderful food we just had.'

Her little, sincere prayer was so precious, prompting the rest of us to take turns praying deeper and deeper as we knelt about that new place of prayer. My heart almost burst with joy inside me. 'O God,' I prayed, 'thank You for the joy and privilege of family. Please fill this prayer pouf—our place of prayer—with Yourself. When we kneel here, may we feel You. Fill this whole house with You. Fill us with You.'

And then Chris also prayed asking God to come in a special way to our new place of prayer. Skip prayed next, and after he finished praying, he told us it seemed that a shaft of light came down and surrounded us all.

After Jan closed in prayer, I wondered, *Have I merely replaced the old green chair?* Possibly. But much more than that. This is a place for not only my private praying—*but corporate family prayer!*

It was just five days later that several family members again gathered at the prayer pouf—this time the night before my husband's cancer surgery. The prayers of thanks flowed: 'Thanks for the privilege of a family praying together.' 'Thank You for having taken us through so many hard things—so that we can trust you for Chris' surgery tomorrow.' 'Thanks, Father, that You have never let us down.' Then came the plea, 'Put Your arms around him and hold him close, dear Lord.' Skip's prayer from his medical doctor's perspective was next. 'Protect his mind while he is under anesthesia, please, dear Lord.'

As I reached over and laid a hand on my husband's shoulder and head, I prayed, 'O God, fill him with Yourself. Holy Spirit of God, fill him right now with Your peace, courage, and even Your joy.'

Last, Chris prayed and gave himself completely to God for His will in handling the cancer in his body. And he closed telling God he was so grateful for our family caring and for their prayer support.

That prayer pouf has been the scene of many deep family prayers. I remember my knuckles turning white as Kurt squeezed my hand so hard as we begged God to reveal His will to Kurt for his future career after college. Then later his wife, Margie, newly married to Kurt, was there as all three of us knelt after Kurt and Margie had responded to several mission board invitations at the Urbana Missions Conference. We agonized in prayer for God to show them if He wanted them on the foreign field or to stay in America.

When my only sister Maxine, and her husband, were en route to the Philippines for short-term missions in their retirement, the depth of love and closeness we experienced as we knelt with them at the prayer pouf—sending them off with God enfolding them—was indescribable joy. Another most meaningful time was when Maxine and I—the only remaining members of our immediate family—knelt there and prayed, 'O Lord, pass the mantle of prayer on to our children.'

Home—a place to gather to fellowship. A place to enjoy family meals together. A haven in the storms of life. But, most of all, *a place to pray!*

WHAT FAMILIES ARE ALL ABOUT

Our doctor daughter Jan called one Monday night, sobbing about a problem faced by her husband, also a doctor. 'Skip has a very ominous looking growth on his ring finger.' We spent hours of prayer bombarding God's throne for our Skip. The very next day God, knowing our concern over a fatal type of cancer, gave both Jan and me the same Scripture verse to comfort us: 'The Lord knows the days of the blameless, and their inheritance will be forever' (Ps. 37:18).

Then as our family sat together in our family room, not knowing until the next day that the lab test would show the growth to be benign, Skip began apologizing. He told us he was sorry for putting the whole family through such agony because of a growth on his finger. But our Nancy responded with the essence of our crisscrossing family prayers: 'Skip, that's what prayer is all about. And that's what families are all about.'

CHAPTER THREE

Praying Family Members to Christ

H
AVE YOU WONDERED after you have prayed and prayed and prayed about your children's rebellion, sinful lifestyle, or lack of interest in Christian things why God hasn't answered? Why your children don't live the way you taught them? Why they don't practise a godly lifestyle? It may be they are just searching for independence—or their own personal identity. Or it may be just plain rebellion against God or family standards. However, a likely explanation is that they never *really* received Jesus as their Saviour and Lord. They still have their old nature.

By far the most important prayer to pray for every family member is to receive Jesus as personal Saviour and Lord. Without a genuine salvation experience, your children and other family members are still in the spiritual condition of everybody before they are made alive spiritually by accepting Jesus. Their condition is described in Ephesians 2:1-3:

> And you were dead in your trespasses and sins, in which you formerly walked according to the course of this world,

according to the prince of the power of the air, of the spirit that is now working in the sons of disobedience. Among them we too all formerly lived in the lusts of our flesh, indulging the desires of the flesh and of the mind, and were *by nature the children of wrath,* even as the rest.

Dr. Bruce Wilkinson, president of Walk Through the Bible Ministries, in his 'The Seven Laws of the Learner' series gives these startling statistics about teenagers (in America) today:

- 65 percent of all Christian high school students are sexually active.
- 75 percent of all high school students cheat regularly and think it is OK.
- 30 percent of all high school seniors have shoplifted during the past 30 days.
- 40-50 percent of teenage pregnancies are aborted, the young mothers killing their child.
- 3.3 million teenages are alcoholics (1 in 9).
- 1,000 teenagers try to commit suicide every day.
- Up to 10 percent of high school students either have experimented with homosexual behaviour or are living a homosexual lifestyle.

Dr. Wilkinson went on to list a major national magazine's seven big school problems of 1940 contrasted with today. In 1940 the problems in schools were: talking, chewing gum, making noise, running in the halls, jumping the queue, wearing unsuitable clothing, and not putting paper in the wastepaper basket. Today, however, the seven big school problems are: drug abuse, alcohol abuse, pregnancy, suicide, rape, robbery, and assault.

You are hardly alone if you have a child or children who are not living for God. It is obvious that something is drastically missing today. While it is true that Christians sometimes are guilty of gross sins, could the main reason possibly be that even those who call themselves Christians are really not believers—that they have not received a new

nature and still are living according to their old sinful
nature? Ephesians 2:4-5 goes on with the answer to this
problem:

> But God, being rich in mercy, because of His great love with
> which He loved us, even when we were dead in our trans-
> gressions, made us alive together with Christ (by grace you
> have been saved).

To have a child or any family member living a godly
lifestyle, the prayer we must pray first is for him to have
Jesus living in him as Saviour and Lord. In themselves,
family members never will be able to live godly lives, or
even have the desire to do so. A real salvation experience
actually makes us new creations in Jesus. Second Corinthians 5:17 explains this new being that we become:

> Therefore if any man is in Christ, he is a new creature; old
> things are passed away; behold, all things are become new
> (AV).

IS IT A REAL SALVATION EXPERIENCE?

The church our family has attended during vacations for
over forty years had a tremendous shock not long ago. The
son of one of their finest families had as a lad seemingly
received Jesus, been baptized, and had participated as part
of the church family for years. Then he went into military
service and steadily moved farther and farther away from
God, ending up on drugs and in trouble with the police. A
definite wedge developed between him and his whole family
as time went on.

Coming home from the service with a wife and new
family and facing his mother who suffered with life-threatening cancer, he got into more trouble and ended up in
prison. It was then that he realized that his life was empty
and hopeless and his claim to knowing Jesus was not real.

Soon after that he stood before the congregation of his
boyhood church and told them that, though he had gone

through all the proper steps, he really had not become a genuine Christian as a lad. But now, he said, he really had received Jesus as his Saviour and Lord of his life. 'I want you all to know that I love the Lord,' he testified as he requested to be re-baptized—this time as a real believer. The stunned church congregation watched as he stepped into the baptismal waters for his first *believer's* baptism along with his young wife, a new Christian. It was a baptismal service the congregation would long remember.

Jesus said to Nicodemus, 'Truly, truly, I say to you, unless one is *born again*, he cannot see the kingdom of God....Do not marvel that I said to you, "You must be born again" ' (John 3:3, 7, italics added). It is frightening to even consider that any of our own children—or other family members—may not be truly saved, born again.

A close friend has been a pastor of liturgical churches all his adult life. Having just retired, he told me he is going to write another book, this one about the many, many young people he watched go through their confirmation classes, memorize all the right Scriptures, and correctly answer all the questions. 'But as soon as confirmation was completed,' he said, 'that's the last the church saw of many of them.' Then he sadly added, 'These, I firmly believe, never had a real experience of salvation.'

My only brother, Edward, evidently was one of those, though no one but God knows for sure if his childhood profession of faith was genuine or not, or knows whether it was just peer pressure, family prodding, or just the honest good intentions of a young boy—but nothing more. Edward seemed to be such an eager little Christian, passing out Gospel tracts and being so faithful at church. But then peer pressure in junior high school and the temptations of tobacco and alcohol won out. Within a few more years it was the wild lifestyle of a travelling highway contractor, three wives, a prison term for accidentally shooting a girlfriend to death, and finally deciding there wasn't a God at all.

Had he really received Jesus—or was it just the church environment in which Mother kept us? Or was it just, as a boy, doing what everybody in his young church social group was doing? We'll never know. But for thirty years He lived completely away from God, even denouncing His existence.

It took thirty years of agonizing, persistent, daily prayer by our mother—and much prayer by the rest of us. And then it took a near-fatal accident to bring him to Jesus—for the last two years of his life here on earth.

No matter how long it takes, their personal salvation should be the number one prayer that we pray for each of our children and family members.

REPENT AND BELIEVE

As I talk with parents, I realize children turning their backs on all they have been taught is a very common occurrence. One overseas missionary, agonizing over her own teenage daughter's rebellion and plans to marry a communist, told me she believed that many young people brought up in the church really haven't had a valid experience of salvation. They went through the proper classes, passed with their buddies, joined the church with the group. 'But was there ever real repentance and acceptance of Jesus not only as Saviour but as their Lord?' she asked me. She answered her own question with a sad, 'I think not.'

Why is this so? It takes more than the head knowledge of believing that Jesus is the Son of God. Even the demons do that, but they certainly aren't saved. Somehow we have reduced becoming a Christian to only accepting intellectually what the demons believe—that Jesus the Son of God came to earth, died on the cross, and rose again the third day. It takes more than that. Many have forgotten that Jesus started His preaching with 'repent and believe' (Mark 1:15) and have lost the fact that the early church immediately was built on both repenting and believing in Jesus (see Acts 2:38). Then after Peter explained to the believers in

Jerusalem that God had called him to bring Jesus to the Gentiles too, they replied: 'Well, then, God has granted to the Gentiles also the *repentance* that leads to life' (Acts 11:18, italics added).

During the hours before I received Jesus as my Saviour, I was miserable. The evangelist had preached about everybody needing his or her sins forgiven, and I, as a nine-year-old child, had cried all afternoon over my sins. My mother and new-Christian older sister, Maxine, hovered over me like midwives—expectant, eager for the new birth. They spent hours instructing, answering my questions, and explaining my terrible burden of guilt. But when that preacher finally ended his evening sermon and gave an invitation to come forward and receive Jesus, I was the first to shoot out of my seat. As I knelt repenting, with our Sunday School superintendent at my side, the guilt was swept away. And as I prayed for Jesus to come into my heart, I knew I was a Christian—ecstatic, thrilled, born again, *forgiven!*

> For He [God] delivered us from the domain of darkness, and transferred us to the kingdom of His beloved Son, in whom we have redemption, *the forgiveness of sins* (Col. 1:13-14, italics added).

So, what should we pray for our unsaved family members? Pray that they will see their sinful condition, repent, and truly receive Jesus as their Saviour.

THE MATTER OF RIGHT BIRTH CIRCUMSTANCES

There are many rites of passage methods into church membership and Christianity that may or may not produce real Christians. A church staff member, the mother of a daughter approaching adolescence, said to me recently: 'I am scheduled to go away for further theological education next year, but I don't think I should go. That is the year my daughter will be the "right age" to go through the church's membership class, and I need to be home to supervise her entrance into Christianity.' Shocked, I wondered where in her previous theological training had she missed that becoming a real Christian is more than being the 'right age' to enter Christianity through a church class?

Then there are those who believe that *where* we are born makes us a Buddhist, Muslim, Christian, or whatever. I have actually had people say to me in all sincerity that they knew they were Christians because they were born in Christian America. That is no more true than the old cliche that being born in a zoo makes us an elephant.

Also, the widespread belief that being born into the 'right family' automatically produces Christians is not New Testament teaching. When Jesus said, 'You must be born again' to Nicodemus, he was talking to one who was a Pharisee and a ruler of the Jews, a follower of Jesus' own religion. Jesus even looked at the religious leaders of His own church who did not believe on Him and said, 'What makes you think *you* will escape the sentence of hell?' (Matt. 23:33, italics added)

An honest look into Christian families reveals that many members are not true believers, born again and destined for heaven.

My own father rested all his life on what his parents' church had done to him as a baby. All of our prodding and twenty-five years of praying for him to receive Jesus and change his extremely worldly lifestyle brought no results—until his doctors told him he was dying. After calling his clergyman (whom he never even had met) to administer last rites, he said to my mother, 'There's more to it than this, isn't there?'

'Do you think so?' she gently countered.

'Yes. Call your pastor.' And my dad received Jesus. Surprisingly, he lived two more years as an invalid, but frequently with his Bible open on his lap, communicating with His newfound Lord Jesus. It took twenty-five years of

persistent prayer for his salvation—and we are so glad that
we never gave up!

INDIVIDUAL BELIEF A SCRIPTURAL MUST

In His conversation with Nicodemus, Jesus insisted on a
personal, individual acceptance of Him as Saviour and
Lord. He said, 'For God so loved the world, that He gave
His only begotten Son, that *whoever* believes in Him should
not perish but have everlasting life' (John 3:16, italics
added).

I recall how the emphasis of a personal salvation in my
presentation affected so many in a large seminar I con-
ducted some years ago in South Africa. Most of those in
attendance were church members who assumed they were
Christians because they had been born into the 'right family,' one affiliated with a certain denomination. However,
after I invited listeners who were not sure they knew Jesus
personally to pray aloud in their groups, attending
denominational leaders were shocked when about seven-
eighths of that audience prayed to make Jesus their personal Saviour and Lord.

Their belief stemmed from the teaching of 'household
salvation'—that is, that the decision of the head of the
household brings salvation to the members of the household. However, God's Word does not teach 'household
salvation.' When the Philippian jailer cried out, 'What
must I do to be saved?' Paul and Silas replied, 'Believe in
the Lord Jesus, and you will be saved—you and your
household' (Acts 16:30-31, NIV). But a careful reading of the
passage indicates that all members of his household were
old enough to believe: 'The jailer...was filled with joy
because he had come to believe in God—he and his whole
family' (16:34, NIV).

The same explanation applies to the account of Cornelius who was promised by an angel that 'you will be
saved, you and all your household' (Acts 11:14). However,
earlier, the Bible says that Cornelius was a 'devout

man...*who feared God with all his household*' (Acts 10:2, italics added). So, *all* the members of his household already were old enough to fear (reverence) God. This could not have included babies and young children, who themselves must personally receive Christ in order to be born again when they are mature enough to believe and fear or reverence God. Faithful praying on the part of believing members of a household can be a means of working in the hearts of young family members calling them to personal salvation. (See pages 59-60 regarding how God cares for young children before they reach an age of accountability.)

'HOW CAN I BE SURE, MOTHER?'
It was our daughter Jan's first child. She searched my face for an answer as she asked, 'Mother, how can I be absolutely sure Jenna will be saved and go to heaven with me?'

'You can't be absolutely sure, darling,' I replied. 'God gave your precious little baby a *free will* just as He gave everybody else on earth.'

With tears in her eyes she cried, 'What can I do then? Can't I do *anything* about it?'

'Oh, yes, Jan, there are many things you can, and must, do. First you yourself must *live* your Jesus in front of her every minute. In all you do and say, she must see Jesus living in you. You must teach her the things of God and surround her with music and stories about Jesus. You must keep her enfolded in a good church family.'

This is what Chris and I promised God we would do at the important time of dedicating our infants—but really ourselves—to God.

'But, Jan, by far the most important thing you will do for her is *pray*. Pray continually that she will find Jesus as soon as she is old enough to understand. Although God gave Jenna a free will, He will move in her heart in proportion to your praying. Pray, pray, pray!

'No one can make that decision for your child, not even you, her parent. Even Jesus didn't assume that authority over anybody. Although Jesus wept over Jerusalem, longing to gather them to Himself, they would not. Although those He was weeping over were born into Jewish families, they chose not to follow Jesus. Nothing you can do, Jan, will guarantee that Jenna will go to heaven. *That is strictly a personal decision every person must make—no matter who their parents are or what ritual or rite of passage they have gone through.'*

And the prayers for Jenna's salvation were answered. While Jenna was still at playschool, as her parents were praying together with her at bedtime, she prayed so sweetly and sincerely, 'Jesus forgive my sins and come into my heart.'

TRAIN UP A CHILD

What about 'train up a child in the way he should go, and when he is old he will not depart from it' (Prov. 22:6)? I have had many parents almost defensively say to me, 'But I *have* trained up my child in the way he/she should go. So why isn't he/she living a Christian life?'

First, that verse doesn't say that the child will *never* go through the 'prodigal son' stage, rebelling against God and family. It says 'when he is *old* he will not depart from it.' That explains temporary 'departings'.

Also, I have been astounded at the lifestyle of some parents who honestly believed they had brought up their children 'the way they should go'. Their gods had been money, careers, social status, or pleasures instead of the godly lifestyle the Bible dictates. Examples in the home of self-centredness instead of the biblical caring for others, amassing treasure on earth instead of heaven, putting the body above the soul in priorities—all directed the child away from, instead of toward, God.

But there are Christian households in which children *are* trained to go God's way, and the children still go wrong. There is no apparent condemnation of the New Testament father whose son became the famous prodigal. Therefore, believing parents who have faithfully trained their children in the way they should go should not feel they are failures. Once I was discussing these matters with our daughter Nancy. She commented, 'Mother, the danger of a good Christian home is that the children learn to say all the right things and learn all the right Scriptures—but they may never internalize them into their own lives. And they may never make their salvation personal.'

When parents have done the very best they could, but the children turn their backs on everything the parents hold dear, rebel against all that has been taught them, and pick friends that horrify the parents—it is time to re-evaluate their child's actual relationship with Jesus. Of course, this may be just their cutting the apron strings or trying their wings to find out who they are. But it is important to make sure your child actually has the *new nature* the Bible promises:

> For by these He has granted to us His precious and magnificent promises, in order that by them you might become *partakers of the divine nature*, having escaped the corruption that is in the world by lust (2 Peter 1:4, italics added).

THE PRAYER FOR SALVATION

Yes, the prayer for salvation is the most important prayer I, as her mother, prayed for Jan and her sister, Nancy, and brother, Kurt. I persisted, frequently agonized in prayer, until I had listened to each of my three children invite Jesus into their lives. It also was the most important prayer my mother prayed for me.

I remember the family prayers that brought me to Jesus. I was born into a family that knew nothing about this personal relationship with Jesus. In fact, my family knew little of Jesus Himself. But when my mother trusted Jesus as her Saviour when we were young children, her first thought was for our salvation too.

Nobody taught my mother to pray. There were no prayer seminars and 'how to' books available to her. She just listened to the older saints in Wednesday night prayer

meetings—and started to pray. And her first prayers were
for her children's and her husband's salvation. As mentioned earlier, I was only nine years old, but it was my
mother's zeal for Jesus and fervency of her prayer that
brought results that very year.

Never question if it is right to pray for a family member's
salvation. The Bible clearly says that 'God...desires all
men to be saved and to come to the knowledge of the truth'
(1 Tim. 2:3-4). And again, 'The Lord...is patient toward
you, not wishing for any to perish but for all to come to
repentance' (2 Peter 3:9).

Although Paul apparently never married, it was for his
whole extended Jewish family that he said that his 'heart's
desire and my prayer to God' was for their salvation (Rom.
10:1). And I have joined Paul in making this the number
one prayer for my whole extended family too.

Have you made it your prayer for your family?

HOW OLD MUST A CHILD BE TO COME TO CHRIST?

The age a child can understand he or she needs sins forgiven and Jesus as Saviour varies tremendously depending
on his or her training and exposure to Jesus. There are steps
in a child's development starting at grasping 'Jesus loves
me' to the ultimate awareness of being a sinner and needing
the Saviour.

My son-in-love Skip reinforced that needing a Saviour
from their sins develops at different times in children.
'There are tears in my eyes,' he said to me, 'when I think
back to our Crista saying when she was just twenty-two
months old, "I love Jesus." Then when she was just three-
and-a-half-years old, after listening to a Bible story on a
James Dobson radio programme, her spontaneous and
unprompted prayer was, "I'm sorry, God, for breaking
Your rules."' It was just two days later in church that she
had her dad write a note and put it in the offering plate
saying, 'I love Jesus...(signed) Crista.' And after falling

asleep that Easter night, she opened her eyes and said, 'He is risen,' and went back to sleep. *Her Saviour!*

Crista's own father was a little boy when he sat on the knee of the child evangelist and received Jesus—again the product of praying parents who cared enough for lost souls to have started in their living room a now-thriving church.

The concept of doing wrong may develop earlier in a child than we expect, and we must keep alert to make sure we help children translate that into receiving Jesus when it is time.

A NUTURING ENVIRONMENT

It happened very early in Jan, Crista's mother, our oldest child, too. It was two months before Jan's fourth birthday when I found her facing the wall on her bed, crying. She had just listened to her father preach through an Easter series of sermons. When I asked her what was wrong, she sobbed out that 'the awful, awful naughty things' she had done had hung Jesus on that cross.

Sensing immediately that God clearly was dealing with her, although I hadn't dreamed she had started to understand, I gently led Jan through the prayer of asking God to forgive all those bad things she had done—and then asking Jesus to come into her heart and be her Saviour. It was one of the most definite, and thrilling, salvation prayers I ever have heard—and it's still holding to this day! God answered my prayers much more quickly than I had expected.

One of the greatest days of my life as a mother was when I had the unbelievable joy of praying with my last child, Kurt, as he asked Jesus into his heart as a seven-year-old. *All of my children saved!*

My husband, Chris, had received Jesus at the same age as he and his parents were returning home after his mother had preached an evangelistic sermon in a mission. Young Chris asked his father to stop the car because he wanted to ask Jesus into his life. For years young Chris had heard his father pray fervently for him and for the lost people his parents were trying to reach for Jesus. And, repeatedly, young Chris had heard his mother explain in their meetings how to become a Christian.

In relation to Kurt's coming to Christ, his dad had preached the Gospel in his hearing. And I had prayed every day while Kurt was in my womb, and after he was born I had rocked him to sleep with songs about Jesus. As with our other children also, I had prayed at his crib every night until he was ready for me to pray *with* him. So our son also was ready—ready to bow his head with his parents and receive Jesus as his Saviour, as his own dad had done at age seven.

MAKING SURE
Our second child, Nancy, also prayed with me asking Jesus into her heart while she was at nursery school, but she remembers a step she took later. She definitely felt she already was a Christian, and clearly remembers talking to God in prayer. In fact, she told me, she remembers praying a lot with her Grandma Moss, frequently saying, 'Father, if there is anything in my life that is wrong, forgive me.' But at age eight she attended a kid's evangelistic meeting and felt she needed assurance of salvation. She then rededicated her life to Jesus. 'The "re" was important, Mother,' she told me. 'I didn't question my salvation, but that day I cemented it.'

This step often is necessary when children have made their first commitment to Jesus early. Some really might not have been mature enough, and this actually is their initial accepting of Jesus. And, even though it was a sincere first prayer, more maturity is frequently needed for the child to understand completely the meaning of making Jesus not only Saviour but the Lord of his or her life.

Also, there are children who do not reach that 'age of accountability' or spiritual maturity until later in primary school or perhaps in secondary school. But it is never too early to start the praying for children to find Jesus as their Saviour. Yes, the prayers for our children's salvation started before their births—and continued until God answered.

PRAYING FOR GRANDCHILDREN

I have grandchildren, but God does not. He only has children. We only can become the children—sons and daughters—of God, not His grandchildren.

> But as many as received Him [Jesus], to them He gave the right to become the children of God, even to those who believe in His name (John 1:12).

My prayers for the ultimate salvation of my grandchildren started before they were born, and mingled together with their own parents' prayers. So the prayers for these precious little ones entrusted by God into my children's families multiplied and multiplied until one by one they have received Jesus.

Our son-in-love Dan told me that their Cindy (our first grandchild) definitely reached the 'age of accountability' at four. She had a deep understanding that there was a God who sent His Son Jesus into the world to die for her own sins. And she knew she needed to ask forgiveness for her own sins, and very emphatically prayed that prayer with her daddy.

'She was our ponderer, our thinker,' Dan said. She understood the good and the bad guys in the universe, and wanted to make the choice for God. One day she said, 'Daddy, I have Jesus in my heart now. Satan can't hurt me any more.'

Cindy and her sister Kathy had a lot of early training about Jesus both from their parents and the Christian playschool they attended. From the time they could talk, the school taught those little ones a simple Bible verse for every letter of the alphabet—beginning with 'A is for "All have sinned" ' and 'B is for "Believe on the Lord Jesus Christ and thou shalt be saved." ' Through the alphabet they memorized the steps of salvation, the essence of Christianity, and a child's responsibility. I remember how surprised I was when three-year-old Kathy rattled off all those verses for me plus Psalm 23 and dozens of songs about Jesus.

They also learned to pray honestly to God as their Friend at playschool. So it was natural for Kathy to receive Jesus as her Saviour, repeating her prayer a couple of times to make sure. Then while still three she popped up in Sunday School and clearly explained that Jesus was living in her heart—the concept that seemed to stick best in her little mind.

No matter how young or old your child is, it is important to start praying now that when your child is ready, he or she will receive Christ.

EVEN BEFORE THEY UNDERSTAND?

A close friend was following the casket that held the body of one of her triplets. 'That's my baby; that's my baby in there,' she sobbed.

'Mother, will you talk with her?' our Jan begged. 'People are telling her that her baby will be in hell eternally.'

It was a deep privilege to talk with her about our own four babies, who I thoroughly expect to be waiting for us in heaven; to explain to her that I am sure my two unborns lost in miscarriages, my full-term stillborn, and my seven-month-old Judy (too young to understand when she died) are in heaven with Jesus! Why am I sure? Because David so definitely said about his dead child, the son born to Bathsheba, 'I shall go to him, but he will not return to me' (2 Sam. 12:23). And:

> They were bringing...babies to Him [Jesus] so that He might touch them, but when the disciples saw it, they began rebuking them. But Jesus called for them saying, 'Permit the children to come to Me, and do not hinder them, for the kingdom of God belongs to such as these' (Luke 18:16).

These Scripture passages make me know that I, with David, will be able to go to my infant offspring too. And, if my two small grandsons' lives here on earth were to end before they could understand accepting Jesus, I know our James and Brett will join us in heaven too.

A DYING MOTHER'S LETTERS

It isn't only for a better and holier lifestyle here on earth that we pray for our family members to receive Jesus. Their salvation also determines their eternal destiny—either in heaven or hell.

My mother had a clear biblical picture of every one of her family members without Jesus being forever in hell (Rev. 20:15). Her consuming passion was their salvation. I wept as I read two letters my mother wrote while I was at secondary school. One was to my father and one to us three children written on the eve of her very serious surgery. It was the same surgery that had taken her mother's life, and somehow she was convinced that it would take hers too. Here are what she thought were her final words, written in the hospital, to my unsaved dad:

> To My Dearest:
> As I am facing an operation I do not know but perhaps it might be God's will to take me home that way, so I want to tell you that I am very happy in the Lord and am resting on His precious promises.
>
> I have prayed much for you, my dear, that you might be saved. I love you so. I feel that God has spoken to you many times through sickness in our family, and now once more He is speaking. It may take the life of one precious to you before your eyes will be fully opened; but, dear, I gladly give my life if it will be the means of your salvation. Just ask Pastor Larson or any good Christian to show you the way, and I will be waiting for you on the other side. To know Him is life eternal. You will find several salvation texts in the front page of my Bible. Read them and believe them.
>
> If I must leave you, my darling, I hope you can find a good Christian woman to come in and keep house. The

children will need someone to mother them and to continually remind them to keep looking up, to keep praying, and no matter what happens to just put their whole trust in Him who died for them.

Do not let my going hurt you so that you give up, darling, but rather give thanks to God that you have found your Lord and that you know we shall meet again and be together for all eternity.

Yes, the most important prayer to pray for our family members is for their eternal salvation!

CHAPTER FOUR

How to Pray When Loved Ones Hurt

MOST PRAYERS FOR FAMILY members are uttered because someone in the family is hurting. It is watching our loved ones suffer that drives us to our knees, begging God to intervene. Sometimes God's answer comes immediately, the hurt is handled, and a quick 'thank-You' finishes it. But there are other times when the problem causing the hurt persists—hours, days, even years. How do we pray then?

In the Bible I received for my eighteenth birthday from my then boyfriend, Chris, I underlined in red God's answer to that question in Hebrews 11:6—*faith!*

> And without faith it is impossible to please Him, for he who comes to God must believe that He is, and that He is a rewarder of those who seek Him.

And through all these years it has been God's rule for my praying—*in faith.*

FAITH THAT IS TRIED

But sometimes the depth of the suffering or the duration of
the need severely tries our faith. I'll never forget how my
daily prayers deepened in intensity month after month as
our entire family prayed for our son-in-law Dan Thompson
when he lost his job for refusing to lie to Congress about the
irregularities he discovered in the books of the Farm Credit
Administration, for whom he worked as a financial analyst.
As previously mentioned, he could not find another financial position despite the fact the national Merit Systems
Protection Board had ruled six months later in Dan's
favour—all because his former employer had appealed the
case. Dan and Nancy were plunged into a nightmare.

As I prayed during the early weeks of this ordeal, I began
to feel a gnawing fear for Dan's reputation and future
forming in the pit of my stomach. One night I was awake,
pleading with God for several hours. The next morning I
knelt at my prayer pouf several more hours, imploring God
to bring truth and justice to the situation. Early the following morning I was desperate. As I picked up my Bible, I
prayed, 'Father, I *must* have an answer. Please—*today!*'
With tears in my eyes, I began reading devotionally in Luke
8 at the story of Jairus.

Jairus, a ruler of the synagogue, was entreating Jesus to
come to his house because his twelve-year-old daughter was
dying. But when a messenger came with the news that his
daughter already was dead, what Jesus said to Jairus
almost jumped off the page at me:

> Don't be afraid any longer; only believe, and she will be
> made well (Luke 8:50).

I cried out, 'O God, I believe Dan will be healed.
Increase my faith.'

The fear suddenly evaporated, vanished, lifted from me
like a heavy cloud. Yes, the problem was still there, but my
heart soared as I wrote *'promise!'* in the margin of my Bible.

I couldn't wait to phone Dan and tell him what God had promised me, and was disappointed when Dan was not at home. But God didn't want me to tell him—He wanted to tell him Himself! That same day, God gave Dan the very same verse, and in shock we compared notes that evening. The message—that was to carry us for three-and-a-half years—came from God almost simultaneously to both of us 1,000 miles apart: 'Only believe!' *Have faith!*

FAITH REMOVES FEAR

I was reading in the New American Standard Bible, and two explanatory words have been added after Jesus said, 'Do not be afraid.' They are 'any longer.'

Jesus is not surprised at human fear when we are encountering the unknown, facing a calamity, anticipating excruciating pain, or experiencing a devastating disaster. Jesus understood the fear in that father's heart—and in mine. I remained kneeling in silence several minutes, engulfed by the wonder of my Lord, overwhelmed at how He understood my human frailty. The tears turned to praise and thankfulness—and worship of my wonderful Lord.

That was the end of my fear. Although the problem was not solved for three-and-a-half more years, that fear didn't rear its ugly head again. 'Don't be afraid any longer!' said Jesus. 'I'm here!'

It was a whole year later, still in the midst of the devastating problem, that Jesus summed it up when He gave John 16:33 to me for Dan and Nancy:

> These things I have spoken to you, that in Me you may have peace. In the world you have tribulation, but take courage; I have overcome the world.

BASE FAITH ON SCRIPTURE

It is important to base our faith, not on our own whims and wants, but on what God says in the Bible. Faith is not blind faith in what we ourselves decide we want. It is faith in what God says to us in His Word, the Bible. It is God giving us His doctrine, reproof, correction, and instruction in righteousness (2 Tim. 3:16) out of the Bible that forms the basis of what we pray in faith.

The Jairus promise was just one Scripture, although a very important one, that God gave for Dan and Nancy. There was a three-and-a-half-year running account of promises, warnings, and instructions. Here are a couple of examples of a specific Scripture for a specific need at a specific time:

In May 1988 while Dan was struggling in prayer and rationalizing whether or not he should expose the financial discrepancies, God gave me Ephesians 5:11 for him:

> Do not participate in the unfruitful deeds of darkness, but instead even *expose* them (italics added).

And just before that, God had given Jesus' position on truth out of John 3:20-21:

> For everyone who does evil hates the light, and does not come to the light, lest his deeds should be exposed. But he who practices the truth comes to the light, that his deeds may be manifested as having been wrought in God.

It is human nature to pray for things to come out all in our favour—whether we deserve it or not. But prayer doesn't allow that, for it is petition to God. And His treatment of His creatures conforms to the purity of His innermost nature. Justice is a fundamental quality of God—the revelation of His holiness.

Through those years I never had the freedom to pray anything for the outcome of Dan's problem except justice. God would not let me pray, 'Restore everything to Dan— income, his reputation, his job.' Rather the Holy Spirit led me to pray, 'Father, You alone know all the facts. Know which things Dan actually does deserve to have restored—

and if there are some he doesn't. Lord, we want only Your all-knowing justice.'

> Does God pervert justice or does the Almighty pervert that which is right? (Job 8:3)

Jesus clearly stated the answer in John 5:30:

> I can do nothing on My own initiative, as I hear, I judge; and My judgment is just; because I do not seek My own will, but the will of Him who sent Me.

God used innumerable Scriptures about His justice to instruct and encourage us, including passages stating that those who do the wrong will receive the consequences without partiality (Col. 3:25), and God will give relief to the afflicted when Jesus returns (2 Thes. 1:7). 'Who will bring a charge against God's elect? It is God who justifies' (Rom. 8:33). *God's justice!*

I still have all the Bibles I have used in devotions since I was eighteen, with dates and notes of what the Lord had for me to pray right then. Through my fifty years of marriage, God always has given me exactly what and how He wanted me to pray—for myself and my family members. And when He said it, I have stepped out, confidently or shakily, praying in faith.

ENCOURAGEMENT FROM OTHERS TOO

Members of my United Prayer Ministries board prayed for Dan all those years, too, and God gave them Scripture verses for him as well. Amazingly, those who were going through the deepest trials with their own families often were the ones God gave the most insightful Scriptures for Dan and Nancy. One member, whose heart was still breaking over her own daughter who disappeared just before completing her medical studies, taking her two daughters with her, sent this incredible promise to Dan:

God will not reject a man of integrity, nor will He support the evildoers. He will yet fill your mouth with laughter, and your lips with shouting (Job 8:20-21).

Another board member's daughter had a baby out of wedlock, for years kept running away, dealing in drugs, and then vanishing for weeks with the infant, or leaving the baby with its alcoholic father, who abused the child with cigarette burns. The board member's verses from God to Dan were:

'And they will fight against you, but they will not overcome you, for I am with you to deliver you,' declares the Lord (Jer. 1:19).

'For I know the plans that I have for you,' declares the Lord, 'plans for welfare and not for calamity to give you a future and a hope' (Jer. 29:11).

'But,' said that board member, 'all that trouble increased our faith. And we really learned to hang on to God in faith and pray without ceasing.' Then smiling, she said, 'But God has answered all those prayers of faith. Our daughter now is an honours student in her third year of college.'

Most of my board members have had deep hurts in their families. So it was from personal experience that they decided on November 7, 1988, before Dan had any ruling from the Merit Board, that this was God's Scripture for him:

And indeed, all who desire to live godly in Christ Jesus will be persecuted. But evil men and impostors will proceed from bad to worse, deceiving and being deceived. You, however, continue in the things you have learned and become convinced of, knowing from whom you have learned them; and that from childhood you have known the sacred writings (2 Tim. 3:12-15)

But my board members didn't just pull out a Scripture

verse they thought fit. Oh, no. They had learned to wait on God for His words in their own hurts, so they waited on God for Dan's too. And then month after month at board meetings, and daily as I sent through specific needs on our telephone prayer chain, their current Scriptures formed the basis of their praying.

People from all over the United States also phoned or wrote to assure us they were praying. One seminar chairman not only prayed for months, but contacted her US senator about the injustice.

Some dear friends, whose own bank president son-in-law is spending time in prison after a questionable ruling by a judge, called to say they were claiming Psalm 25:1-3 for Dan:

> To Thee, O Lord, I lift up my soul. O my God, in Thee I trust. Do not let me be ashamed; do not let my enemies exult over me. Indeed, none of those who wait for Thee will be ashamed; those who deal treacherously without cause will be ashamed.

PRAYING IN FAITH FOR OTHER FAMILY MEMBERS

When I was praying and God gave me the Jairus promise for Dan, I also was in intense prayer for our son, Kurt, and his wife, Margie, who were making a decision that would affect his whole career. Just finishing his doctoral studies in physics, Kurt was struggling over his next step. Kurt, Margie, and I all had knelt several times together by the living room prayer pouf asking God to direct them clearly, and it had been a deep subject of prayer for them and all of us for a long time. That morning my prayers for Dan and Kurt were mixed, and God knew I needed the 'faith' promise for both. After praying, 'O God, I believe Dan will be healed. Increase my faith,' I immediately added, 'I *believe* you will send Kurt and Margie where You want them!' *Faith!*

Our family members have hurt in many ways. God gave the word *faith* when our Jan and Skip had been married ten years, and still desperately wanted their first baby. After years of their praying (and mine) for our daughter to be able to conceive, I was reading in Hebrews 11, the Bible's great faith chapter. It surprised me that after the passage emphasized the faith of Sarah's husband, Abraham, the list of males of faith abruptly changed to a female's faith— Sarah's. And, as that verse quickened my heart, my own faith soared.

> By faith even Sarah herself received ability to conceive, even beyond the proper time of life, since *she* considered Him faithful who had promised (v. 11, italics added).

This was added to the wonderful promise God had given to Jan's husband, Skip, just as he had to Abraham, Sarah's husband. And our son too had clung to God's promise with unshakable faith.

WHEN FAITH DOES NOT SEEM REWARDED

It is important to read all of that Hebrews faith chapter in the Bible because there were many other Old Testament heroes of the faith who, although they had gained approval through their faith, did not receive what was promised. Some were tortured, stoned, mocked, scourged, chained and imprisoned, put to death, afflicted, ill-treated, and even sawn in two (vv. 35-39). They did not see the promise.

Not all of our prayers of faith have been answered the way we wanted them here on earth, either. The biblical reasons are many. Dan had felt strongly that God, in His waiting to give answers to our prayers, was teaching us. We have discovered that to be true in our family trials through the years. (Chapter 6 of this book will mention the things God was teaching our family while He was silent during our praying in times of trouble.)

Most importantly, the time for the proof of our faith is coming.

> In this you greatly rejoice, even though now for a little

while, if necessary, you have been distressed by various trials, that the *proof of your faith*, being more precious than gold which is perishable, even though tested by fire, may be found to result in praise and glory and honour at the revelation of Jesus Christ (1 Peter 1:6-7, italics added).

FAITH IN WHAT—OR WHOM?

In what—or whom—do we put our faith when praying? Faith in our ability to have faith? Faith in the words printed on a page of the Bible? No. The faith must be in the God who gave the Bible's promises.

Jesus interrupted his interaction with Jairus to give a tremendous visual lesson about the object of our faith—Himself. A woman with an issue of blood for twelve years had come up behind Him and touched the hem of His cloak. Immediately her bleeding stopped. Although the crowd was pressing around Him, Jesus demanded to know who had touched Him in the special way that He felt power go out of Himself. When the woman fell trembling at His feet declaring why she had touched Him, Jesus explained what had healed her—her faith in Him—even the simple act of touching the hem of His garment.

> Daughter, your faith has made you well; go in peace (Luke 8:48).

This prepared Jairus to receive his simple 'only believe' from Jesus. The Lord had just proved before the eyes of the mourners that He had power over physical problems. And, although the mourners scoffed without faith, Jairus and his wife had the thrill of watching Jesus take their dead daughter's hand, telling her to arise. And her spirit returned to her—resuscitated. The result of faith!

Through the years of seeing God answer family prayers in our hurts makes it easier for us to have faith in God too. Four years ago, as mentioned earlier, a doctor found a small growth in my husband. But even before we received the results of the biopsy telling us it was cancerous, Chris and I both prayed together that night, 'Thank You, God, that You never have let us down in all our deep things. This could be one of the worst we have to face, but it is so good to be able to trust You completely for our future. Thank You, Lord, for this assurance we both have tonight.'

Knowing God's identity is an important part of our praying in faith. After we received the biopsy result of 'cancer,' our daughter-in-love Margie sent the following Scripture to us uttered by Jeremiah calling to the Lord from the depths of the pit. She reminded us that this hope can bring us through every trial if we will only call it to mind:

> Yet this I call to mind and therefore I hope: Because of the Lord's great love we are not consumed, for His compassions never fail. They are new every morning; great is Your faithfulness. I say to myself, 'The Lord is my portion; therefore I will wait for Him.' The Lord is good to those whose hope is in Him (Lam. 3:21-25, NIV).

Then it was Margie who gave these same verses to our Nancy when she was behind in her studying for her nursing qualifications because her daughter Kathy had broken her leg—and Nancy herself had been in a car accident the day before, causing her back and neck to ache, this in addition to deep nausea that morning. *Faith in God—producing hope.*

Yes, our faith begins and develops in our Lord—not ourselves.

> Fixing our eyes on Jesus, the author and perfecter of faith....Consider Him...so that you may not grow weary and lose heart (Heb. 12:2, 4).

PERSEVERE IN PRAYER
No, praying in faith doesn't necessarily bring instantaneous results. Many of our family problems have persisted for long periods of time—while we persisted in prayer. Sometimes it is hours, such as the three hours each of two consecutive nights while Kurt took the entrance tests for his

physics doctoral studies. And when I became sleepy after just the first hour of praying, God shook me with Jesus' words in the Garden of Gethsemene, 'What, could you not watch with Me *one* hour?'

Sometimes it is persevering consecutive days such as when our Jan, ten days overdue with her first child, took her medical board exams for eight hours two days in a row. Before starting, I had wondered how I would be able to stay in prayer that long, but the Lord kept reminding me, 'Pray now for her aching shoulders as she bends so long over those papers.' Or, 'She's cold.' 'Pray for clarity of mind.' 'The day is getting too long.' Then, 'Pray for Me [God] to take My holy hands and lift that heavy burden pressing in her womb.' The next day Jan and I compared notes as to what times she had needed those specific things. And, to our amazement, every one was exactly when God had told me to pray!

But most of the time our persisting prayer is for those ongoing, day-by-day nagging troubles that trouble a family. Jesus taught us a valuable lesson about keeping on praying in His parable of a family situation where the unjust judge gave in to the widow's request because she kept bothering him so much.

> Now He was telling them a parable to show that at all times they ought to pray and *not to lose heart* (Luke 18:1, italics added).

Every family member does not get equal prayertime each day—reciting by rote each name during a formal prayertime. Our praying for each other is in proportion to the need of each. There are times one family member requires concentrated prayer from us right then—sickness, surgery, giving birth, danger, unfair treatment, emotional or spiritual needs.

Much of the time it is those immediate, imperative situations that demand our prayer at the time. On the first day of Dan's Merit Board hearing in August 1988, most of our family was on vacation on the shores of Lake Michigan. We promised Dan that would be our day of prayer, and there was much individual prayer and at meals. But in the afternoon we gathered in the shallow water to pray. Jan was on the big yellow lilo as Skip knelt on one side and I on the other with the waves lapping over our feet. Chris came and stood in the water as we all prayed for Dan.

That morning Skip had spent time studying biblical truth and justice in his devotions, and he formed the words first. 'Truth and justice is what I am praying, Lord.' The same words were mine. 'Jesus, give the judge eyes to see the truth. May justice, only justice, prevail. Not unfair settlements. Just justice.' One after the other prayed that prayer. Then we prayed for clarity of mind as Dan testified. For peace. For God's arms to be around Dan.

The next month when ABC national television interviewed Dan in the office of US Senator Grassley, chairman of the Senate Investigating Committee, my grandniece Kirsten and I knelt at the living room prayer pouf and poured out our hearts to God. We prayed for God to make Dan Christlike, that people would see only Jesus in him. We prayed for great wisdom from God. 'Take away all thoughts *he* thinks he should say. Put in his mind, Holy Spirit, exactly the words *You* want him to say. Protect his mind. Keep it clear, sharp. Keep his attitude Christlike at all times. Please!'

Then Kirsten prayed for Nancy—for her peace, her physical needs, her nervousness, her tension. Then I prayed for God to come into her whole being and fill her with Himself.

Later the prayer was for God to protect every word Dan had said. To keep *truth* there, not the way the news media sometimes twists things.

WHEN WE DON'T WANT TO PRAY

When a family hurt drags on for weeks, months, and even years, it is hard to keep on praying as instructed in Ephesians 6:18:

> With all prayer and petition pray at all times in the Spirit, and with this in view, be on the alert with all *perseverance* and petition for all the saints (italics added).

Dan's wife, our Nancy, ran out of patience several times. 'Mom, I just prayed, "Do something, God!" '

When the pressure got too great, Dan even admitted getting angry with God a couple of times, praying much as the psalmist often prayed. 'God, You *can* do something. Why *don't* You? Why are You so silent—so long?'

I remember one day sagging under the ongoing load of so much praying, and complaining, 'Lord, I'm sick and tired of praying these prayers!' And I was. That kind of prayer is hard work. And I was tired.

I felt that these attitudes were sinful. Being able to confess them melted those fleeting negative feelings, and we settled into the regular prayer routine again.

WHEN WE DON'T KNOW WHAT TO PRAY

The day after our family had prayed for Dan on the beach, I had a surprise. At 5:45 a.m. I tried to pray for him, but my utterances were just perfunctory words. I would pray for other family members, and then come back to Dan again. But still nothing. At 8 o'clock I finally said, 'Lord, I don't know how to pray for Dan today. There is nothing there. After hours of wrestling in prayer for him yesterday, I just don't understand it.'

Finally, after praying about my own cleansing and any other hindrance I could think of, I blurted out, 'Father, I don't know how to pray for Dan today. Holy Spirit, please pray *for* me. Romans 8:26-27 is where I am today.' Then I recited the passage:

And in the same way the Spirit also helps our weakness; for
we do not know how to pray as we should, but the Spirit
Himself intercedes for us with groanings too deep for words;
and He who searches the hearts knows what the mind of the
Spirit is, because He intercedes for the saints according to
the will of God.

Then the Holy Spirit took over, and for fifteen minutes
He prayed. I formed no words except 'Dan' and 'Holy
Spirit' for the entire time. What a precious relief!

ELEVENTH-HOUR ANSWERS

Some time later Dan was at our summer cottage. Looking
up from his dinner plate, Dan asked, 'Why does God so
frequently wait until the eleventh hour to answer, when He
knows all along how He is going to answer when we pray
about a problem?' He shook his head and wondered aloud,
'Why am I still making mortgage payments on two houses
with no income?'

'I've struggled a lot with that one, Dan,' I replied. 'In
fact, I'm questioning having the right to write a book on
family prayers with such a big one still outstanding in our
own family.'

Why did God wait until the very last minute to rescue
Peter when Herod was about to kill him just as he had killed
the Apostle James—in spite of so much prayer being made
for Peter?

And on the *very night* when Herod was about to bring him
forward, Peter was sleeping between two soldiers, bound
with two chains....And behold, an angel of the Lord suddenly appeared, and a light shone in the cell; and he struck
Peter's side, saying, 'Get up quickly.' And his chains fell off
his hands (Acts 12:6-7, italics added).

We have had intermediate eleventh-hour answers too
numerous to mention, but the big one came the very night
before I was scheduled to start writing this chapter. I had

resigned myself to having to report that we are still in the
waiting stage—*in faith*. Perhaps, I thought, it was God's
will for us to be waiting because so many Christians reading
this book would be in that same situation in their family
prayer life. But God wanted the victory to be written in this
chapter—our faith rewarded!

As I was about to begin writing this chapter on praying
in faith for loved ones when they hurt, I was still in North
Carolina after a speaking engagement. When I called home
that night, Chris just exploded the good news over the
phone. 'Dan won his case! The Merit Board has not only
upheld its first decision but has cleared Dan's name completely—and actually praised him for his stand and integrity.'

The Associated Press put it succinctly in a news release:

> A Farm Credit Administration (FCA) employee who
> refused to lie to Congress was back at work Monday, three
> years after a judge ruled he had been fired illegally.
>   Daniel J. Thompson was fired in May 1988 after he
> accused the agency of destroying internal studies [Dan's]
> that showed the Farm Credit System was in deeper financial
> straits than its then-chairman...wanted to reveal to Con-
> gress.

Then the AP quoted Senator Grassley, who headed the
government's investigation:

> It's obvious Thompson was wrongly fired, and it's also clear
> that Congress got incomplete information four years ago
> [when Congress approved a $4 billion bailout of the sys-
> tem]. As the court order states, he was fired in retaliation
> because the information would have been embarrassing to
> the chairman of the FCA.

The press release concluded:

> Grassley said Thompson has been awarded back pay, but

'this alone cannot make up for all that he has lost because he elected to be forthright and honest.'

When your family members hurt—*pray in faith. It works!*

CHAPTER FIVE

How to Pray When Loved Ones Hurt Us

A YOUNG WOMAN sought me out at a convention. 'I am a psychiatric nurse with a master's degree and just have been offered a full scholarship for a doctorate at a good university,' she began. 'God has told me to ask you to pray for me about whether or not it is something I should accept.' As she told me about her success with some of the most difficult patients, I realized she knew the dimension that is frequently missing in this field — *God*. She adds prayer, making her very needed and uniquely qualified to help victims.

Here is one of her experiences that convinced me. 'I was assigned a violent psychiatric patient who had not shaved for fourteen years, with a tangled beard down to his waist. He had hurt so many caregivers that nobody wanted to go in his hospital room, and he hadn't let anybody touch him all that time. Fourteen years ago his family, not being able to get him to change something wrong in his life, agreed with a counsellor that what he needed was an "intervention procedure". So his family had gathered and pounced on him, brutally accusing him and exposing his wrongdoing. It so shocked him that he snapped mentally—and he has been in this condition in that psychiatric hospital ever since.

'But,' the nurse continued, '*I am a Christian. And I prayed and prayed about that man.* Finally, ignoring his fierce threats of "You know I can really hurt you," I walked into his room and began a slow process of tenderly working through his hardened shell—while I prayed. And,' she bubbled, 'it *is* working. He gradually has let me touch his hand—and even pray for him!'

Assuming someone in his family was a believer and could have prayed for him, what part could prayer have played if it had been applied earlier in the handling of this man's wrongdoing? What might have been avoided if God had been included fourteen years earlier? How would God, in response to their praying, have given divine wisdom to those seeking to help that erring family member? If they really had followed God, He could have added His reproof, healing, reconciliation, and restoration of this family's oneness again.

When a family relationship is ruptured that badly, is a lifetime like that inevitable for the victim? Or could prayer—then and even now—help?

PRAYER—WHEN WE HAVE BEEN HURT?

The hardest time to pray about family matters is when we have been hurt by loved ones. All of us are wounded from time to time by those we love (and certainly we all also wound loved ones). I do not believe there is any person who has escaped being hurt at some time within his or her own family. Even Jesus' own kinsmen must have hurt Him immensely when they came to take custody of Him 'because He had lost His senses' (Mark 3:21).

This hurting by loved ones usually is unintentional, and frequently the family members are unaware they have wounded each other. Most of these hurts result from thoughtless acts, words, omissions, or neglect. In the close proximity of families, we accidentally step on each other's toes so easily.

Then there are those times when the words or actions have been with the best of intentions, but have backfired, causing deep wounds in our family members.

And, of course, there are those times when the motive for hurting another family member is revenge—or feeling justified in using some cruel means to accomplish an end the family member has decided must be accomplished. And even when the criticism is deserved, the pain could have been avoided had it been handled in a less hurtful way.

Occasionally, there are those shattering hurts from other family members that absolutely devastate people. They render their victims unable to cope with everyday living (like the man with the fourteen-year beard), leave them bitter, not caring or, in extreme cases, not even wanting to live. At those times their motive or reason for hurting doesn't seem to count. Whether it was deliberate or unintentional, for our good or theirs, doesn't enter into our thinking. And it certainly doesn't ease the immediate pain.

I'm by nature a hugger. I constantly reach out to hurting people in my ministry. But I vividly remember saying once after I'd been deeply hurt by several family members, 'It hurts too much to hug them—with this knife sticking in my back.'

HOW DO WE PRAY WHEN WE HAVE BEEN HURT?

Pray? How are we able to pray at those times when we feel betrayed, excluded from their intimate communication, even unwanted? How do we pray while we are just barely treading water ourselves? Or, how do we pray when the little everyday hurts just chip away at us?

It is not the being hurt, but what we *do* with the hurt that will determine our future relationship with that family member.

Prayers at these times can be what keeps a family

together. Neglecting to pray, and to pray the right kinds of prayers, almost insures a family split of some kind—physical or at least emotional. *The prayers we pray will determine our future relationship with the family members who hurt us.*

WHAT DO WE PRAY?

There are many prayer *steps of prayer* in the family healing process.

A particularly devastating confrontation in our extended family clearly reminded me of these steps. Immediately after it took place, I had to leave for an important speaking assignment in a college in a neighbouring state. Completely shattered, I crawled into the bed in the back of our van and desperately cried out to God as my husband drove me to the meeting two-and-a-half hours away. I wept as I prayed. 'Lord, what should I do? How should I handle this?' How should I, could I, pray? I begged, 'Lord, please give me the attitude *You* want me to have. Other advice can be so confusing, so conflicting, and sometimes so wrong. But never *Your* advice!' I sobbed. 'How do I pray when I am bleeding this hard?'

As a result of my prayertime in the van, I began to focus again on the forgiving formula from 2 Corinthians 2:5-11 that I had taught and used personally hundreds of times. I sorted through those points one by one: forgive, comfort, and reaffirm your love—in order that Satan cannot take advantage of the situation. Out of this experience I outlined eight prayers that we should pray when we are hurt by loved ones.

● *Prayer No. 1—'Lord, change me.'* God answered me by immediately bringing to my mind that I first should ask the Lord to search my heart and enable me to change my attitude toward the loved ones who had hurt me. I was not surprised. God had taught me that secret for living with others twenty-three years before, and I had written about it in my second book, *Lord, Change Me!* It is the prayer I have prayed more often than any other, frequently several times in a day. And here it was again. Me!

For the first two hours in that van I wept and agonized in prayer, crying, 'O Lord, change *me*; change *me!*' 'Forgive *me*, Father, for everything that is *my* fault. Lord, make *me* absolutely clean before You!'

It was two hours of Psalm 139:23-24:

> Search me, O God, and know my heart;
> Try me and know my anxious thoughts;
> And see if there be any hurtful way in me,
> And lead me in the everlasting way.

'Lord, forgive me for retaliating verbally,' I pleaded. 'Lord, cleanse me from my ugly reactions and un-Christlike attitudes.' (Through the ensuing months, I recorded innumerable tear-filled prayers of 'Lord, change me' as steps of the incident unfolded.)

But only when I felt in that van that I had my own attitudes and my relationship with God in order was I ready to turn to my relationship with those who had hurt me. This sequence is crucial. It is impossible for us humans to forgive others until we have settled our own relationship with our Heavenly Father.

● *Prayer No. 2— 'Lord, help me forgive.'* The most important prayer in the whole family healing process is prayer that leads to our being able to forgive loved ones—not just in words but truly in our hearts.

So, that last half hour of the trip I spent asking God to help me forgive those family members who had so wounded me. And I did—immediately, within hours after I had been hurt!

I was right back to Jesus' words that I have taught so often in seminars for over twenty years to everybody else. In Matthew 6:14-15 and Mark 11:24 Jesus said that if we forgive others, God will forgive us; but if we don't, He won't! Jesus said it didn't do any good for me to pray those two and a half hours asking God to forgive me if I wasn't willing to forgive also!

I wondered if God had brought Jesus' words to Stephen's mind when he forgave the people who were hurting—and killing—him, the first martyr for Jesus (see Acts 6:8-7:60). It was a scene of terror as the angry mob gnashed their teeth at Stephen, snarling like a pack of attacking dogs. And when he gazed intently into heaven and told them he saw the glory of God and Jesus standing at His right hand, they exploded. Covering their ears, the whole snarling mob erupted into terrifying yells. Shouting, they pushed and shoved Stephen out of the city, and suddenly he felt the stabbing pains of stones crashing against his whole body. Knowing he was dying, Stephen cried out, 'Lord Jesus, receive my spirit!' But the remarkable part of Stephen's response to their anger is his dying request. Falling to his knees, he shouted above the angry mob, 'Lord, do not hold this sin against them!' How similar to his Saviour's dying words on the cross, 'Father, forgive them for they know not what they do!' The secret—*forgiving*.

Many families have gone through times when the bitter words, shouted accusations, and snarling attacks felt like the sharp stones that mutilated Stephen. In most of my seminars, I listen to devastated family members spill out similar horror stories.

So what do we do when family members hurt us? We first settle our own relationship with God, letting Him prepare us and give us the ability to forgive (which may take considerable time). And then, as I in my heart did in that van, we fall before God and forgive.

Jesus put a high priority on being reconciled. If you remember that a fellow believer has something against you when you are giving your offering, first go and be reconciled before you present your offering. God doesn't even want our money if we aren't willing to forgive and be reconciled: 'First be reconciled to your brother, and then come and present your offering' (Matt. 5:24). And Jesus warns that

God will punish those who, having been forgiven themselves, refuse to forgive someone else: 'So shall My Heavenly Father...[punish] you, if each of you does not forgive his brother from his heart' (Matt. 18:35).

I was surprised to find out from a 'Dear Abby' newspaper column that there is an annual International Forgiveness Week at the end of each January. Abby gave this beautiful thought from George Roemisch:

> Forgiveness is the fragrance of the violet that clings fast to the heel that crushed it.

Forgiving does not mean that we condone what people have done. And it does not absolve the sinner of accountability to God—or responsibility to the one hurt. *Forgiving is the step God, in His omniscient wisdom, provided the victim, to heal his hurt, mend the relationship, and restore the God-intended unity in family relationships.*

● *Prayer No. 3— 'Lord, help me comfort those who hurt me.'* In addition to praying 'Lord, change me' and to enable you to forgive, the next step is to pray to be able to comfort those who have hurt you. The Apostle Paul wrote about treatment of 'any [who] has caused sorrow...forgive and comfort him' (2 Cor. 2:5, 7).

Early one morning at my prayer pouf, I randomly had turned to the story of the end of Joseph's life in Genesis 50. After Joseph's brothers had sold him into slavery, they were starving in a famine, and God used Joseph to rescue them. The brothers who had hurt him worried, 'What if Joseph should bear a grudge against us and pay us back in full for all the wrong which we did to him?' What if Joseph hadn't forgiven them? And I wrote in the margin of my Bible, 'What if I should hold a grudge?' What would happen?

But Joseph calmed their fears by saying, 'Do not be afraid.' Joseph had no intention of retaliating. He had forgiven his brothers for being so unfaithful and mean to him. Then he comforted them by speaking kindly to them.

Suddenly hot tears blinded my eyes. This is to be *my* attitude! Months before I had decided no accusing confrontation until some touchy circumstances cleared themselves. But now God confirmed that comforting and speaking kindly was to be my attitude *always*. I mentally considered each of the family members involved, resolving that there would be no attitude of retaliation toward any of them—ever. And the peace of God settled in all around me.

● *Prayer No. 4—'Lord, enable me to pray for those who hurt me.'* When loved ones hurt us, we must pray *for* them, not just *about* them. Praying for them not only involves God in their healing process, it changes us also while and because we pray. Jesus said, 'But I say unto you, love your enemies, and *pray for those who persecute you*' (Matt. 5:44, italics added).

Immediately after our Dan had illegally lost his government job because of refusing to lie to Congress, his family was praying together about it. There were all kinds of prayers flying up to God concerning their rights, their emotional and financial survival, and God dealing with the agency head who had fired Dan. But suddenly Cindy, their then six-year-old, prayed, 'Dear God, what that naughty man needs is Jesus. Please save him!' She alone had grasped the need to pray *for* the troublemakers. The rest of us had to catch up with her insight in obeying Jesus' words in Matthew 5:44, 'Pray for those who persecute you.'

It is easy to pray telling God 'to get even for us,' 'to heap coals of fire on their heads,' 'to give them what they deserve.' Praying *for* them when they have hurt us is more difficult.

It frequently takes time to come to this place. A local pastor had sexually abused more than a hundred young boys in his churches, and the hurts were incredibly deep. But now, two years later, many of the parents of the victims have finally been healed enough by God to be able to forgive—and now are praying *for* that pastor while he is incarcerated. God has taken them through the stages of grief so necessary to be able to forgive, so that praying for him is possible.

Infidelity is one of the deepest hurts in a family. It isn't easy, for example, for a wife to pray *for* a husband who is having an affair with another woman. But a beautiful, meticulously groomed woman at a seminar handed me a note about how she was praying even for the other woman in her husband's life. 'I'm praying that God will so fill the needs of my husband's girlfriend with Himself that she won't need to be fulfilled by my husband any more.'

● *Prayer No. 5— 'Lord, help me love.'* Again, in His Sermon on the Mount, Jesus included *loving* in His instructions to pray for those who persecute you: '*Love your enemies*, and pray for those who persecute you' (Matt. 5:44, italics added).

A woman at a recent prayer convention told me she was deeply hurt by her son's choice of a wife, and kept praying for the Lord to change her daughter-in-law. Suddenly the woman realized that *she herself* needed to change her own attitudes, so she prayed, 'Lord, give me the *love* You want me to have for my daughter-in-law.' And, she said, that prayer changed things completely!

The prayer 'Fill me with Your love, Lord' has had amazing effects upon me in my family relationships through the years. It has turned my negative attitudes into love for those who have hurt me instead of 'just obeying' Jesus' command to pray for those who have wounded me. It is hard to fathom that such a little prayer could have such profound effects.

The Bible's warnings to Christians in 1 John about *not* loving are truly frightening:

> By this the children of God and the children of the devil are obvious: anyone who does not practice righteousness is not of God, nor the one who does not love his brother (3:10).

> If someone says, 'I love God,' and hates his brother, he is a

liar; for the one who does not love his brother whom he has seen cannot love God whom he has not seen (4:20).

One of the most precious memories I have is of the late evening one of my daughters and I sat alone in her darkened living room, working out a deep hurt. The rift had come so unexpectedly. Though she had had the best of intentions of fixing a need in our extended family, the situation had suddenly erupted into flying accusations and loved ones vocally defending their own points of view. That night as our time of praying and talking came to an end, we sat with our arms entwined around each other. The tears streamed down our faces and mingled into one as we murmured over and over, 'I love you, Mama'/'I love you, darling.'

Loving each other is the powerful glue that holds our families together.

> And beyond all these things, put on love, which is the *perfect bond of unity* (Col. 3:1, italics added).

● *Prayer No. 6—'Lord, enable us to pray together.'* If at all possible, set up a time to pray *with* the family member who has hurt you. Or quickly take advantage of any opportunity to turn your discussing, arguing, or humanly trying to resolve the differences into prayer.

However, his or her continuing anger, embarrassment, or indifference may make this impossible or even inadvisable. Or he or she may not be ready yet for that depth. But one of the most healing steps in broken family relationships is together inviting the impartial, loving God into the relationship through prayer. His holy presence does wonders in the healing process.

● *Prayer No. 7—'Lord, call others to pray for me—and us.'* There are times when we are so shattered by a family hurt that praying for ourselves, and a family member who has inflicted the hurt, is impossible. Words simply won't come.

This is when the crisscrossing prayers of other family members take over for us.

And this is also when I call my prayer chains. For over twenty years I have had my ministry's board members organized on telephone prayer chains ready to pray for me and my family—and I for them, as previously mentioned. When I send through a prayer request, they don't expect all the gory details—just that I need special, intense prayer right then. It is so wonderful to feel God lift the burden *while* they pray! And it is exciting to watch Him answer—*because* they prayed!

My phone rings several times a week—sometimes a day—with a broken spouse, parent, or child asking us to pray for them because they just can't handle being hurt by a family member. And we always do. But then I encourage them to get into some local prayer group of people who care and will pray for them. Or, if not available, to organize two or three Christians who will faithfully hold them up in prayer through their trial. Or I encourage them to use their church's telephone prayer chain, telling them that having a few pray-ers right around them in ongoing problems produces profound results in the problem—and in them. I know!

WHEN THEY WON'T HUG, WHAT DO WE PRAY?

The ones who hurt us may still feel anger even though we have forgiven them and are praying for them. There are still things about which they may be angry—justifiably or not. Perhaps they have not forgiven us or accepted our forgiveness. Or they may not see their own responsibility for their actions, not feeling there is any initiative they need to take. Or they aren't ready in their healing process to hug yet.

So, what do we do when *they won't hug?* Over that we have no control. We are only required to follow the Bible's admonition in Romans 12:18-19:

If possible, *so far as it depends on you,* be at peace with all men. Never take your own vengeance, beloved, but leave room for the wrath of God, for it is written, *'Vengeance is Mine, I will repay,' says the Lord* (italics added).

'Never take your own vengeance, beloved' is hard, especially when we feel we have done everything we were instructed to do in the Bible, and the hurting still goes on. When unfair words cut into us, when uninvited thoughts of defensiveness pop into our minds, when a martyr complex starts to creep in, it is difficult not to retaliate.

And obeying 'Vengeance is Mine..., says the Lord' is even harder at times like these. Actually practising leaving the matter with God is not easy. But forgetting the 'getting even' and retaliating, and leaving the justice to God is our only hope for reconciliation in family squabbles and hurts.

I've learned an amazing secret. Many years ago during a hurtful Christenson family situation, the Lord relentlessly kept bringing to my mind, 'Vengeance is Mine..., says the Lord.' Then I found myself *praying* it back to Him over and over and over. In such situations, that repeated prayer almost miraculously changes *my* attitudes and feelings. I no longer need to retaliate—or lick my wounds. And I am able to settle back in peace.

● *Prayer No. 8—'Lord, break the "victim chain." '* Everybody is a victim. Every family member is at times the victim of their other family members during various circumstances. Siblings are frequently victims of their brothers and sisters. Children are victims of their parents. Parents also are victims of their children's actions, words, and attitudes. And their parents are victims of their parents—the grandparents. It goes on and on.

As I chatted about this with a best-selling author/psychologist at a Christian Booksellers Association convention, he remarked, 'Everybody is a victim of a victim of a victim of a victim. All the way back to Adam and Eve. We're *all* victims.'

Standing one day at my father's grave, I did some mathematics on the dates of those buried around him. His father was buried with his three wives! Quickly, I deduced that my father had been deprived of two mothers very young in life. He had been the victim of a very difficult childhood. After his confession to my mother, it had taken me two years to forgive my father for being unfaithful to her, making her (and then me) his victim. But, standing at that grave, I suddenly saw not just myself as *his* victim, but *him* as a victim also. How I wished, too late, that I had understood in my early adulthood when I was so angry with him.

All parents, even though their children may be victims of their sins and inadequacies, also were victims of their parents, who were the victims of their parents.

And more and more we are seeing parents and grandparents becoming a new generation of victims by being blamed by their own 'adult children' for their problems.

Since being a victim is inevitable for us all, is it possible for us to break the victim chain? Does everybody have to keep the 'victim mentality' forever? Does each consecutive generation pile up all their past hurts and keep them in a seething caldron inside of themselves as 'adult children'?

This is where the omniscient, omnipotent God of the universe must take over. His Word, the Bible, has some good advice for us:

> When I was a child, I used to speak as a child, think as a child, reason as a child; when I became a man, I did away with childish things (1 Cor. 13:11).

God deals with us and expects us to deal with problems as adults, if we are. He certainly is not against our past hurts being identified, but never getting to the place of dealing with them as grown-ups is less than God has provided for us. We must come to a place of being accountable to Him and responsible to others for our attitudes. After we grow up, how we eventually handle the hurts is up to us. And how we handle them determines our ultimate healing.

With the Apostle Paul, we can confidently say, 'I can do all things through Christ who strengthens me' (Phil. 4:13).

Prayer is essential here, two kinds of prayer. Much prayer *by* mature Christians brings God's grace and ability to the struggling victim. And time spent *with* God by the victim infuses him or her with the comfort, love, and courage needed to face the problem.

Of course, there are times professional help is absolutely necessary to identify of whom and how they have been victims—especially when the brain has protectingly blocked out the extreme pain and abuse of a childhood trauma. Professional help may be needed to get to the root of a person's current troubles, especially if he or she has been a victim of physical, emotional, mental, or sexual abuse.

Identifying the problem is a necessary step, *but identifying does not heal*. And living and forever wallowing in the new-found information may only compound the problem. So, once that has been established, how does one change into a happy, productive, spiritually healed adult?

The big word in this procedure is *forgive*. Only when genuine forgiveness has taken place can the real healing process take place. The healing process seems to take time in proportion to the hurt. And it is a *process*. There is a grieving process when the loss has been large. But the *turning point* is forgiving.

Judy Rae's (not her real name) process has taken many years. When I wrote her story of horrible child abuse in my book *What Happens When God Answers*, I did not know the complete story. As her memory has returned through years of counselling by professionals and a wise and caring pastor and wife, plus years of intensive prayers for her, the surfaced facts are horrendous. She was the daughter of Satan-worshipping parents who sexually abused her over the years. And as soon as she was old enough, she was forced to have six babies—all of whom were sacrificed to Satan.

Once she was made to plunge the dagger into her own child!

A few months ago I was chatting with that pastor's wife about Judy Rae. She said, 'With her master's degree, Judy now is a counsellor in our new psychiatric hospital here. They say they could not get along without her; she's so great with these victims.'

'When do you feel her turning point came?' I asked.

'Oh, there's no doubt about it. When she forgave!'

I pushed a little further. 'Was it the time she called me screaming over the phone asking if what I said Jesus said (in a seminar) was true? When I said that now that she is a Christian, if she doesn't forgive, God won't forgive the sins she commits as a Christian either? (Matt. 6:14-15) And she had bought my *Gaining Through Losing* book, and I told her there was a chapter in there that would show her what would happen to *her* if *she* didn't forgive? And then she called back happily saying she had forgiven them and called again to say she had phoned her family to tell them she had forgiven them—and to ask them to forgive her for her unforgiving spirit so many years?'

'That was the time,' the pastor's wife answered. 'And the big change came when she called her parents and told them!'

It was good to learn so many years later that forgiving really had worked. There often is just a temporary smoothing over of feelings or even burying them again—but this was real!

Forgiving is not as much for the sake of the one forgiven as for the victim. A recent note from a seminar attendee says it so clearly:

> I was a victim of incest, but when I accepted Jesus, my father persecuted me. When I was an adult, God convicted me of my hatred of my father. When I forgave him, later he was saved. Shortly after that he died.
>
> I have been feeling proud that God had healed me, but today (at the 'Lord, Change Me' seminar) I realized I had

not forgiven my mother for being an accessory, for not protecting me. I have now forgiven her, and Jesus has healed me of this also. Jesus is still the Great Physician!

In India I walked into an amazing home just swarming with happy, polite, loving girls and boys who squeezed and squeezed me as I left. The 'parents' of this home currently have 300 drug addict children from the streets and hundreds more they are teaching. Astonished, I ask the 'mother' how they all turned out so well. She explained, 'They have gone through the most horrible experiences for years with nobody to look after them, begging to eat, sleeping on the train platform and being routinely sexually abused, we pick them up from the train platform. And,' she added, *we never talk about their past*. We just love them, accept them unconditionally into our family, *pray much, introduce them to Jesus—and He heals them!*'

What can help snap that victim chain? Yes, forgetting the past, reach out for the joy that Christ gives. Philippians 3:13-14 wisely tells us: 'But one thing I do: *forgetting what lies behind and reaching forward to what lies ahead*. I press on toward the goal for the prize of the upward call of God in Christ Jesus' (italics added).

A woman in California whose face just radiated told me a horror story of family abuse from when she was two years old. 'But now I run a home for victims of family abuse,' she continued. When I asked her about the transformation in her life, she beamed. 'When I accepted Jesus, He made me a new creation in Himself' (see 2 Cor. 5:17).

Yes, this applies even though victims may harbour extreme guilt, feeling the abuse was somehow their fault. But if that victim has come to Christ for salvation, he or she must realize that God has not only forgiven past sins (see Col. 1:13-14) but also is willing to lift all the undeserved feelings of guilt: 'In whatever our heart condemns us…God is greater than our heart, and knows all things' (1 John 3:20).

SALVATION PRAYER

These eight prayer steps work. They have worked for me and my family; they can work for you. First, however, there may be a prayer you must pray—'Lord, make me one of Your children. Forgive all my sins, and, Jesus, come in as my personal Saviour and Lord.' All of God's promises for healing were not written to everybody—just to those who have received Jesus as personal Saviour and Lord. If you have read this far and have not yet received Him into your life, it is imperative in the healing process to make sure that you, the victim, are a real Christian with Christ living in you. You can 'do all things through Christ' only if you truly belong to Him.

Trusting Jesus as Saviour does not guarantee all problems will immediately disappear, but it does guarantee the emotional, mental, and spiritual healing process of the Great Physician.

STEPHEN'S SECRETS

When we are disillusioned, hurt, or even horrified at the words or actions of a family member, we must have the attitude of Stephen who, when he was being stoned to death at the hands of the angry mob, was 'full of grace and power'. How did he stay so calm in the midst of such an assault? How can we?

The answer is twofold. First, Stephen had supernatural help. He knew Jesus personally as his Saviour and certainly as Lord of his life. Then Stephen was full of the Holy Spirit before the attack began. It was not just human grit, heroism, or bravery while they were stoning him to death. It was the omniscient God of the universe filling Him. And we can have the same experience.

The second secret of Stephen that can be ours is his seeing Jesus. Today Jesus is looking down at our hurts too. Keeping our eyes on Him, not other humans, will provide that supernatural courage and strength we need so desperately in devastating family times.

When we are disillusioned, hurt, or even horrified at the

words or actions of a family member, the greatest lesson we too can learn is to *keep our eyes on Jesus!* He never will let us down or disappoint us. He will never give us wrong advice. And He never will withhold all we need to cope with our family problems.

CHAPTER SIX

'What Are You Teaching Us, Lord?'

'Ev, DO YOU REMEMBER the first thing you said when I told you your little seven-month-old Judy was dead?' John Carlson, the chairman of the board of my husband's first pastorate, recently asked me. Whatever, it was I had said had not stayed in my reeling, grieving brain. No, I couldn't remember. John looked at me with a still-lingering slight shock as he reminded me that I had reacted to the death of our baby with, *'I wonder what God is trying to teach us now.'*

Judy's seven months of surgeries and paralysis from the waist down had ended with our watching her slowly die in the hospital.

It had been Chris's turn in the hospital with our little Judy when she went to heaven. And John had come home with him to break the news to me.

Then I had questioned, 'God, why teach us *again?*' Hadn't we learned enough through the first miscarriage, then our full-term stillborn baby girl, and then another miscarriage? Why another baby's death?

Then John said I had mumbled, more to myself than to

96

him, 'I guess if I'm going to be a pastor's wife, I'm going to have to know some of these things.'

GOD'S METHOD OF TEACHING

During the summer after Chris completed his studies, I had prayed and prayed for God to teach me how to be a pastor's wife. With trepidation in my heart at such a huge task looming in front of me, I sat at the feet of a pastor's wife I deeply respected, gleaning every speck of advice I could get. But God added His divine teaching.

I had been pregnant with Judy in 1952 when Chris went to his first church, but I certainly didn't understand that Judy's death was one of the ways He was really preparing me for the years ahead of that task.

It was over twenty-five years after Judy's death that I was on a California radio talk show and a woman called in from the East Coast. There wasn't a dry eye in the studio after she said to me, 'I'm a Christian today because of watching you at my little sister's casket. When I was a little girl my baby sister died, and you and Pastor Chris came home from your vacation to have her funeral. Mrs Chris, all you did at that mortuary was hold my mother in your arms and cry. And I remember saying to myself, "If that's what a Christian is, I want to be one." And I am.'

It was March 23, 1971 while studying in John 15:7 about Jesus' promise of astounding prayer power that I prayed, 'Lord, I want that power in prayer. *Teach me and break me until I have it.*' Little did I realize that the way I would experience that power was in actually praying. And that it basically would be our family needs and difficulties that would keep this wife, mother, mother-in-law, and grandmother on her knees—wrestling, interceding, releasing.

Yes, I have experienced that tremendous power in prayer in a round-the-world prayer ministry. But I also have experienced the teaching, and the breaking, it has taken for God to answer that prayer for prayer power.

GOD'S METHOD OF ANSWERING FAMILY PRAYERS

Also, when I pray for God to improve some attitude or action in one of my family members, I often am surprised at His method of answering my prayers. Frequently, He accomplishes that for which I have prayed not by supernaturally sprinkling them with sweetness and goodness from heaven, but by answering through a trial.

My mother, after praying almost thirty years for her son to come back to God, finally prayed, 'Lord, do anything you need to Edward to bring him back to You.' But she wasn't prepared for the way God answered that prayer. My brother was struck by a car that was travelling fifty miles an hour. Doctors told our gathered family that he would never regain consciousness, but he did—and, as mentioned earlier, he trusted Jesus in the two years more of life God gave him!

When our very independent teenager Jan went to college, I prayed that God would teach her everything He wanted her to learn. One surprising answer came in a very hard-to-accept discipline. Concentrating on French at secondary school, she had made the language lab tapes for her college class. Nevertheless, everyone, including Jan, was required to spend a designated amount of time sitting in the lab learning from those tapes. Not seeing why she should comply, she ended up with her only first-year B. She told her friends, 'Don't ask my mother to pray for you. She'll pray you right out of all A's.' I had to agree with her exasperation and reasoning, but also realized God was answering my prayer by teaching Jan a lesson of following orders that would prove invaluable as she became a medical doctor.

It is dangerous to pray for a family member to lose his or her cockiness and bitterness unless we are ready for God's way of answering. I did, and found God answering with circumstances that humbled that loved one completely.

The same kind of God's answering came when I prayed

for Him to soften one of my family members who seemed to be becoming harsh and brusque. And I found myself almost wishing I hadn't prayed that prayer. I much prefer to have God sugarcoat my family. But His methods of getting the desired results usually are different.

> Oh, the depth of the riches both of the wisdom and knowledge of God! How unsearchable are His judgments and unfathomable His ways! (Rom. 11:33)

THE ALL-IMPORTANT FAMILY PRAYER

It is still that well-worn prayer question we should pray when calamity strikes. Not 'Lord, *how* can I get out of this?' but 'Lord, *what* can I get out of this?'

When there are hurts in my family, that isn't always an easy prayer for me to pray. The wife, mother, and grandmother in me automatically bristles when my family members hurt. My immediate human reaction is to shoot a 'Remove it, Lord' prayer up to heaven. And then I want to continue to bombard Him with pleas to 'take it away' until He does. But I learned long ago that this frequently is not God's plan for our family.

In my husband's many years of preaching, my constant prayer was for the power of God to fill that sanctuary while he preached. And when he was sick I'd bombard heaven for God to heal him in time to preach. But God had something more important to teach me. I gradually discovered, however, that it was when he was ill, with no human power of his own to go on, that the power of Christ took over— producing the greatest movings of God (see 2 Cor. 12:9-10).

If God does not change our hurtful circumstances when we pray for Him to do so, it most likely means that He has a very important lesson to teach us.

GOD'S METHOD OF TEACHING WHO HE REALLY IS

I remember over twenty years ago one of the most catastrophic events our family has ever faced suddenly striking us. The prayer I prayed is as vivid as if it had been yesterday. 'Dear Father,' I beseeched in the depth of that grief, 'don't take this circumstance away—until we *all* have learned *all* You want us to from it.'

The biggest thing God taught me through the months of that tragedy was to trust him. As the hurts rolled on week after week, I felt more and more like Job in His trials. But it also was with Job that I found my faith in God solidifying until it was immovable and unshakable. It was at Job's lowest point, and mine too, that we both cried out: 'I *know* that my Redeemer liveth!' (Job 19:25, italics added)

It has been in these hard things that God has been able to teach me who He really is.

It is in my family trials that He has taught me that He never makes a mistake, that He comes in proportion to my need, that He really does work all things out for my good—because I love Him and seek to please Him.

When things hurt in my family, God has taught me to cling to the promises He gave us in His Word. Promises of His presence, His comfort, His wisdom, His guidance. *Actually, until God has brought us through the hard things of life, we don't really know if those promises are true or not.*

But it is as I have discovered over and over again that He really *did keep* His promises, that I am able to accept them unconditionally for the current family trial.

A letter from a mother in North Carolina said it so well. 'I just finished reading your *Gaining Through Losing* book, and wept for joy as I read it. The reality of the biblical truth that "fullness of joy" comes through suffering was lost to me until our son Daniel was born without any arms. *The strength, grace, and love the Lord gave me was indeed in proportion to my need. I've known Him in a way that I've never known Him before.* Anything the world has to offer is pale by comparison.'

A woman approached me after a seminar recently. 'I couldn't *stand* your *Gaining Through Losing* book until my sixteen-year-old daughter committed suicide four weeks ago. I grabbed that book and read it over and over. It got me through!' Well, not the book, I reminded her, but the God of that book whose promises she finally had accepted—because for the first time she really needed them.

GOD'S METHOD OF PERFECTING AND MATURING US

When God does not remove painful situations in our families, He is doing something far better than just taking them away. He is in the business of producing mature, deeply spiritual Christian giants of the faith of our family members. What prayers do we pray in times like these? Pray each thing, in order, according to James 1:2-4:

> Consider it all joy, my brethren, when you encounter various trials, knowing that the testing of your faith produces endurance. And let endurance have its perfect result, that you may be perfect and complete, lacking nothing.

Our son Kurt was trying to finish postgraduate studies and was deeply frustrated when the several million dollar electronic microscope he was working on kept breaking down. Having the lens made and remade several times overseas, often waiting up to six months for delivery, he fretted about all the 'wasted time,' swinging from impatience to exasperation. And he and his advisor actually ended up making a lens that finally would work. After wearying from persistent prayer for each specific detail, I suddenly found a new prayer attitude emerging in me from God. He showed me that this was not wasted time—but would be one of the most important parts of Kurt's training.

There was one prayer that God would not let me pray for our daughter. She was pregnant while on those thirty-six-hour hospital shifts of her medical residency. My mother's heart bled for her, and I desperately wanted to pray, 'O God, please, please remove that nausea. She has more than she can handle!' But God restrained my praying with His question, 'How many pregnant women would want her for their doctor if she didn't understand how they felt when they were so sick?'

A military wife in Italy said to me that her husband moved every two years, and each time got a new mistress on that new base. I answered, 'Everybody here has been telling me what a fantastic mother you are and what model Christian children you have. God has been teaching and perfecting you through these incredibly hard circumstances, and has made a beautiful spiritual giant out of you. And I believe one of the reasons is so that you can help the many other military wives going through similar trials to find God sufficient as you did' (see 2 Cor. 1:3-4).

It was almost immediately after Dan's firing from his government job that God powerfully gave Hebrews 2:10 for Dan and Nancy to help us understand that His method of perfecting His children is the same He used for His own Son Jesus—through suffering:

> For it is fitting for Him [the Father], for whom are all things, and through whom are all things, in bringing many sons to glory, *to perfect the author of their salvation* [Jesus] *through sufferings* (italics added).

HURTS BRING US CLOSER TO GOD

The day after Dan lost his job, I was struggling in prayer with several hard things. My spiritual mentor, Kathy Grant, had cancer. Kurt was in the Twin Cities completing the stressful task of making first job contacts. Jan, our doctor daughter, was facing a very undeserved situation at work. That morning I had prayed first about my critical spirit at what seemed so unfair, and finally was able to pray, 'Lord, teach me all I need to know from all of this.' But by evening my prayer had progressed to *thanking God for the tribulations which were bringing me closer to Him*—humbly on my face before Him.

It was Jan who learned that wonderful truth in her physical suffering. It was the first night after the extensive microsurgery which enabled her to conceive Jenna. The pain was excruciating all night. But the next morning she told me, *'I saw Jesus in a way I never saw Him before—in my suffering!'*

Chuck Colson learned this when he was away from all his loved ones the Christmas he spent in prison. I heard him describe how those involved in Watergate as well as several New York Mafia prisoners gathered in John Dean's room in the prison at midnight. Sitting in a small circle on the floor reading aloud from the Scriptures about the birth of Christ, they then prayed quietly for each other—and for their families, most of whom were far away. Although very lonely and cut off from the rest of the world, Chuck added, *'I felt the power of Christ in a way that only comes in times of deepest need.'*

A friend wrote: 'We had hoped to be sending you a birth announcement by now. But our darling baby lived just one week before moving on to heaven. She accomplished so much. She opened our lives to God's endless love, and took us more deeply into life than we had ever been and strengthened our love as a couple. *We thank God for making His loving presence known to us in unmistakable ways during the hardest week of our lives.* He was there in the midst of our pain and fear. He was there as we prayed and wept. And He was there to welcome Katherine into heaven.'

Far away in Cebu in the Philippines, I suddenly felt helplessness and fear about what Dan and Nancy were going through back in the States. Then I read in Mark 6 about Jesus sending His disciples across the stormy sea and, while they strained at the oars, He walked on the water intending to pass them by. But when He saw they were frightened because they thought He was a ghost, He said to them, 'Take courage; it is I, do not be afraid' (Mark 6:50).

The wind stopped when Jesus got in the boat with them.

And I, there in the Philippines, cried, 'O Jesus, get in the boat with us!'

God is teaching us through our family trials not only that they bring us closer to God, but He's also teaching us how faithfully and powerfully He responds to our prayers for Him to come closer to us.

'LORD, TEACH US TRUTH'

One of the things that hurt families—and God—the most is deceit. The Bible is full of warnings and the dire results of deceit. For example: 'The Lord abhors the man of bloodshed and deceit' (Ps. 5:6).

The Bible lumps a lying lifestyle with some very serious sins:

> But for the cowardly and unbelieving and abominable and murderers and immoral persons and sorcerers and idolaters and all liars, their part will be in the lake that burns with fire and brimstone, which is the second death (Rev. 21:8).

Deceit can be either denial or duplicity. In real *denial*, there has been sufficient trauma to cause the brain to bury the truth in order for the victim to cope. But *duplicity*—knowing the truth but lying to protect one's ego, reputation, or actions—is what devastates families.

It is easy to pray for each other when all the family members are living harmoniously—undergirding, fellowshipping, and rejoicing together. But praying for them when there is suspicion and deceit is quite another thing. How do we pray when we believe someone we love dearly is deliberately deceiving us?

First, we pray to know the truth from God ourselves. In family hurts, all members come into the reconciliation process with differing degrees of bias, prejudice, and incomplete or slanted information. And all think they are praying correctly, not realizing their prayers might be wrong.

Second, according to 1 Peter 3:16, when slandered we are

to 'keep a good conscience…in the thing in which we are slandered.' In other words, we are to pray to make sure *we* are pure before God ourselves and acting accordingly.

Third, it is the 'three D's' of deceit, denial, and duplicity that make it difficult for family members to pray in the light of real truth. But, when we are assured of it without a shadow of a doubt, we are ready to ask God to reprove that person as severely as the situation demands. 'O God,' we pray, 'convict them of their sin of deceitfulness, and show them Your truth.'

With the Apostle John, I 'have no greater joy than this, than to hear of my children walking in the truth' (3 John 4). It bubbles up in prayers of joyful thankfulness.

As we drove into their driveway, granddaughters Crista and Jenna were having a heated argument over who got the most magazines in the mail. As Jenna stormed out of the car insisting that one of them had only her name on it, Crista burst into tears. 'She's lying, Grandma!'

'You know something, honey?' I comforted her. 'Do you know who's keeping absolutely true records? Yes, God up in heaven. God knows if *everything* said is a lie or the truth—and He hears *everything*. Truth is truth. And no matter what any person says, you or Jenna, it does not change it one bit. Nobody can change truth into a lie or a lie into truth—just because they say so.'

It was frightening to listen to Chuck Colson quote statistics relating to truth at a Prison Fellowship banquet. When asked if there was any such thing as absolute truth, 67 percent of Americans said no. But even more alarming was that 52 percent of evangelical Christians also said there isn't any absolute truth!

However, not only does God know the truth and record the real facts, Proverbs 12:22 says: 'Lying lips are an abomination to the Lord, but those who deal faithfully are His delight.'

Then Psalm 9:8 says that we don't have to worry about

the final outcome for 'He will execute judgment for the peoples with equity.'

Fully grasping these biblical concepts completely changes our praying—and it changes us. It puts our confidence in God's justice—and us at peace while coping with—and praying for—deceitful family members.

SURPRISE LESSONS WHEN WE ARE DOING THINGS RIGHT

Yes, we all know we learn from our mistakes. But when God chooses to teach us when we are doing what we are supposed to be doing, it's hard for us to understand and accept. Chris and I were not being disobedient to God when we lost our four babies, but God used these experiences to teach us so much. When we lost baby number three, Chris had passed up a glamorous and lucrative piloting job offer in Miami to obey God and go back to college to prepare for serving Him full time. And when Judy died, we had just obeyed His call to enter the pastorate.

> By no means let any of you suffer as a murderer, or thief, or evildoer, or a troublesome meddler; but if anyone suffers as a Christian, let him not feel ashamed, but in that name let him glorify God....Therefore, let those also who suffer according to the will of God entrust their souls to a faithful Creator *in doing what is right* (1 Peter 4:15-16, 19, italics added).

Elizabeth and her husband, Zacharias, were doing everything right when God did not 'take away her disgrace' of being childless until they were advanced in years. According to the Bible, she and Zacharias were doing everything right. 'And they were both righteous in the sight of God, walking blamelessly in all the commandments and requirements of the Lord' (Luke 1:6). But it was after all that sorrowful waiting in barrenness that God sent an angel announcing His intended miracle of the birth of their son John the Baptist (see James 5:10-11).

For what credit is there if, when you sin and are harshly treated, you endure it with patience? But if when you do what is right and suffer for it you patiently endure it, this finds favour with God (1 Peter 2:20).

God delays His answers to our prayers for many reasons, even while we are doing what's right. In the midst of Dan's trials for standing for honesty, God gave us one of His reasons from Hebrews 12:11 which He taught us first when our Judy died—*training us.*

All discipline for the moment seems not to be joyful but sorrowful; yet to those who have been *trained* by it, afterward it yields the peaceful fruit of righteousness (italics added).

God is continuously in the business of making His children into what He wants them to be. And He knows when and how to answer our prayers to make it happen. Cutting short that process by answering our prayers too soon or the way we thought He should deprives us of His divine perfecting.

Through Dan's three-and-a-half years of struggling and waiting because of refusing to be part of a deception, thoughts on 'What Price Integrity?' kept swirling in his head. But 1 Peter 1:6-7 says it is the *proof* of our faith— whether or not we have seen justice here or rejoicing when Jesus comes back:

In this you greatly rejoice, even though now for a little while, if necessary, you have been distressed by various trials, *that the proof of your faith,* being more precious than gold which is perishable, even though tested by fire, may be found to result in praise and glory and honour at the revelation of Jesus Christ (italics added).

In God's waiting to give an answer to our prayers, Dan felt strongly that He was teaching him many things. Here's part of a note Dan penned to me one year into the problem:

I realize that when I reach my limits and feel nothing but utter despair, this problem is inexorably drawing me closer to the Rock. This finding can only be in preparation for a great task ahead. Prayer is changing Nancy's and my hearts. We are both beginning to believe there is light at the end of the tunnel.

WHEN GOD IS SILENT—FROM DAN

Now that the ordeal is over and the verdict of innocent has been returned from the National Merit Board, Dan tells in his own words what God has taught him.

I had questions, so many questions while God was silent those three-and-a-half years. Questions that simmered and sometimes festered in my very being during that long trial.

The question that surfaced first was: *Why me?* Why had I been singled out for all this unfairness and injustice? But God had some powerful Scriptures for me to show me why. The first answer was from John 15:18-20: *because the world persecutes Christians.*

If the world hates you, you know that it has hated Me before it hated you. If you were of the world, the world would love its own; but because you are not of the world, but I chose you out of the world, therefore the world hates you. Remember the word I said to you, 'A slave is not greater than his master.' If they persecuted Me, they will persecute you.

My 'why me?' question was also answered by God showing me that *Christians are called to be different.* Not only was I to *oppose* evil deeds, but I was to *expose* those evil deeds I had uncovered:

> Do not participate in the unfruitful deeds of darkness, but instead even expose them (Eph. 5:11).

Another question I asked many, many times as the months dragged into years was: *Why hasn't God answered my prayers yet?*

Assurance from Him that *I was still to wait, patiently*, came from God in Psalm 62:1-2:

My soul waits in silence for God only; from Him is my salvation. He only is my rock and my salvation, my stronghold; I shall not be greatly shaken.

Becoming desperate at God's silence, I finally agonized over this question: *Am I so stubborn that God must put me through the fire to mold me?*

God's answer to that in John 15:1-2, 8 revealed some 'whys' — *that God may be glorified when I bear much fruit and prove myself to be Jesus' disciple.* No question about it, I was being tested — pruned — for the end result.

I am the true vine, and My Father is the vinedresser. Every branch in Me that does not bear fruit, He takes away; and every branch that bears fruit, He prunes it, that it may bear more fruit.... By this My Father is glorified, that you bear much fruit, and so prove to be My disciples.

Another category of God's teaching came when, even without my questions, the Lord taught me incredible lessons throughout those years. One very important one was *the re-examining of my life's priorities.* God sent me back to the Scripture which was the basis of my life and the foundation on which Nancy and I chose to build our marriage.

Choose for yourselves today whom you will serve...but as for me and my house, we will serve the Lord (Josh. 24:15).

And then, after I had got the clear picture of whom I was serving, God comforted me with one of the most important lessons of my life: *'If God is for us, who is against us?'* (Rom. 8:31, italics added)

God also taught me that He *demands obedience,* but He *honours righteousness with a promise.* What an affirmation of my refusal to compromise my integrity. Job 8:20-21 says, 'God will not reject a man of integrity, nor will He support the evildoers. He will yet fill your mouth with laughter, and your lips with shouting.'

Perhaps the most important lesson I learned was to *trust*

God for all my family's needs—because He is in control. Financially, it was very grim for us. I spent many sleepless nights wondering how I was going to feed and clothe my little ones. But I learned to trust God—and He never let us down. Every single need was met—in time.

> Do not be anxious then, saying, 'What shall we eat?' or, 'What shall we drink?' or, 'With what shall we clothe ourselves?' For all these things the Gentiles eagerly seek; for your Heavenly Father knows that you need all these things. But seek first His kingdom, and His righteousness; and all these things shall be added to you (Matt. 6:31-33).

The third category of things God taught me was *the importance of living with God's love in my life's personal relationships with others.*

Each day brought challenges and opportunities to let Jesus shine through me to others. And a new *meekness* that God knew I needed to learn was mine from Matthew 5:5, 'Blessed are the meek, for they shall inherit the earth.'

In my relationship with others, God also taught me that, as a Christian, I *cannot afford to be angry about my circumstances.* It was a shock to realize that I opened myself to the devil if I did: 'Be angry, and yet do not sin; do not let the sun go down on your anger, and do not give the devil an opportunity' (Eph. 4:26-27).

God forcefully taught me that *I cannot love God and harbour hatred towards others,* even those who have tormented me. I have a higher calling!

> Never pay back evil for evil to anyone. Respect what is right in the sight of all men....But if your enemy is hungry, feed him, and if he is thirsty, give him a drink; for in so doing you will heap burning coals upon his head. Do not be overcome by evil, but overcome evil with good (Rom. 12:17, 20-21).

Finally, through my long, hard experience, God taught me *how to live above mediocrity.* As a Christian, I have a higher calling. And God brought it into focus for me through 1 Peter 1:15-16.

But like the Holy One who called you, be holy yourselves also in all your behaviour; because it is written, 'You shall be holy, for I am holy.'

But I could not—did not have to—do it in my own strength. When all human resources within me seemed to fail, I continuously prayed back to God His incredible—and true—promise in Isaiah 40:31.

But they who wait for the Lord shall renew their strength; they shall mount up with wings as eagles; they shall run and not be weary; and they shall walk, and not faint (AV).

Through it all, my prayers were guided and sometimes almost dictated by God—directly to me through His Word. And they were His day-by-day way of patiently and lovingly teaching me all the fabulous lessons He wanted me to learn by my adversity. And while I waited, sometimes impatiently, for Him to answer our prayers for the trial to be over—He wasn't just silent—He was waiting until I had learned all He was teaching me.

And through the fifty years Chris and I have been married, God has taught our whole family His marvellous lessons also—little by little making us what He, from before the foundation of the earth, planned for us to be. Many, many years ago we as a family learned to pray, not just 'Lord, get us out of this adversity,' but 'Lord, teach us what You want us to get out of it.'

CHAPTER SEVEN

Touching Prayers

OUR LITTLE TODDLER granddaughter Crista had a high fever. As I sat holding her on the living room couch, she slept fitfully with her head on my chest. As I pressed my cheek against her silky hair, soft tears trickled down my cheeks, dropping on her head. What was being interchanged? Whatever it was, it was very real and tangible to this grandmother.

Infants who receive loving touches on a regular basis do much better than those who are neglected, researchers have shown. People alone are prone to more stress, anxiety, and illness. Tests have shown that motherless baby monkeys prefer the warm fuzzy stuffed 'mother monkey,' even though it gives them shocks, to the cold wire 'mother' that provides their milk.

I'm a toucher. I often say that more good is accomplished in my touching than in my teaching, because I always reach out to touch in some way. Usually it's a quick, sincere hug, but the response to that touch is overwhelming appreciation.

What really does happen when we touch? Do our arms

around someone simply tell the person we care—or more? Does a touch actually help an ill person recover more quickly, as some research suggests? Does comfort, love, or even power actually go out through a touch?

JESUS AND TOUCHING

People around Jesus knew that something happened when they touched Him. They saw His physical touch open blind eyes and make the lame walk. The woman who had the issue of blood for twelve years touched the hem of His garment and was healed instantly. Also:

> And wherever He entered villages, or cities, or countryside, they were laying the sick in the market places, and entreating Him that they might just touch the fringe of His cloak; *and as many as touched it were being cured* (Mark 6:56, italics added).

ADDING PRAYER ADDS GOD

Though I have learned through the years that much that is good, helpful, and comforting can be transmitted through touching, there is one additional and powerful ingredient available to Christians in their family touching—*God!* When touching adds God by praying, it brings the God of the universe into that physical encounter.

What happens when grandmas and grandchildren hug? Something very tangible passes between them—a love that is special only to them, a bonding that gets stronger with every hug. One of the greatest places for this to happen is that early morning cuddling when a little one, clutching a worn teddy, gropes through the predawn darkness and crawls into the expectant arms in Grandma's warm bed. *But when we add prayer, we add God to those happy occasions.*

While Dan and Nancy were going through the depth of their trial, their children, of course, were sensing the tenseness in the insecurity of it all. When I was spending an extra day with them after a D.C. board meeting, Cindy climbed into Grandma's bed to cuddle one more time. As she fell back to sleep tightly cradled in my arms, I spent the first minutes just enjoying the love that was flowing from me to her. Then I included God in that precious time. Pouring out my heart for her to our Heavenly Father, I asked for each thing I felt she needed right then. Peace. Security. His love flowing into her. *The prayer added God's arms to Grandma's arms encircling her*—divine arms capable of holding her close with His peace, security, love, plus all the other things He knew she needed. I watched as the facial twitchings of waking played on Cindy's face. Then she saw my face, and shining from her eyes and lips was a little 'isn't-this-great?' smile as she snuggled closer. I never miss a day praying for Cindy and every grandchild *long distance*, but this was that awesome touching of my own offspring—while praying.

Another time as we visited Dan and Nancy's family, four-year-old Kathy and I were out of bed whispering so as not to wake up anybody else. At 5 a.m. she had come for her usual cuddle. 'Do you know what Grandma did while you were in my bed?' I asked.

'Yeah,' she said, wrinkling up her face in an enthusiastic smile, 'you cuddled me.'

'Right, but *what else* do you think Grandma did?' Her eyes widened, looking intently into mine for my answer. 'Grandma prayed for you, darling. While I was holding you close I was praying to God for you.'

Her little four-year-old mind was trying to put those two things together. 'What were you praying for me, Grandma?'

First I asked, 'You already have Jesus living in your heart, don't you, Kathy?' With her 'oh, yes' answer, I continued. 'Well, I was praying that Jesus would fill you and make you just like Himself.'

Straightening, she announced with finality, 'It'll never work, Grandma.'

'Why not, Honey?'

'Because He's a boy and I'm a girl!'

Struggling momentarily with that theological impass, I explained, 'Oh, I was praying that Jesus would fill you with all the wonderful things He *is*—such as His love, His joy, and things like that.'

The puzzled look on Kathy's little face melted into a 'that's neat' smile. My eyes never left hers, not wanting to miss a single bit of that new dimension dawning on her.

The same thing had happened the week before when Jan and Skip had an overnight birthday swimming party for me in a motel. After enjoying the pool for hours, we had knelt around one of the beds for a precious prayertime. However, with the children keyed up from the excitement, we played 'musical beds' a few times, and Chris and I finished the night sleeping with two-and-a-half-year-old Crista.

Waking early, I cradled her in my arms as she slept; and that special something passed between us as I prayed for her, our faces almost nose to nose. Her little hand reached out and took my cheek, and then, holding Grandma's face, she drifted in and out of sleep. But every time her eyes would just peep open, looking right into mine just inches away, there would be a sweet 'I-love-you-Grandma' smile. And my smile would say back to her, 'Oh, I love you so much, dear Crista.' *Touching and praying!* It was one of those happy family occasions that seemed so complete in itself. But how much more there was for us when God was added—through prayer.

When little granddaughters stay overnight at our house, they don't sleep in our guest bedroom—no way. There's a 'cosy' of blankets and pillows on the floor on each side of Chris' and my bed. They start the night in bed with Grandma for their 'to be continued bunny stories' and then our prayertime together. Then it's into their cosies for the night. But I know that sooner or later they all will end up back in our big bed.

I'm always awake early spending a couple of hours praying in bed. So I was already praying for our family when Jenna crawled into my side of our bed to finish the night. As I held her in my arms, Jenna quickly drifted off to sleep. But

I was wide awake—and shifted my praying to only her. I held her close and prayed until dawn broke.

What a difference adding God to the cuddling has made. Whenever any of my dear granddaughters—Cindy, Jenna, Crista, or Kathy—have crawled in for a cuddle, I never once have missed the opportunity of adding God—in prayer.

UNHAPPY TIMES

Our doctor daughter Jan was at work in the hospital and ran to meet the stretcher as they wheeled her Jenna into the emergency room the time a dog had almost bitten her nose off. Kneeling beside her, Jan reached her hand under the sheet to hold her child and prayed desperately. And God too reached under that sheet to hold that child close to Himself. And to heal. Miraculously, as mentioned earlier, there is virtually no visible sign of a scar!

Cindy had several weeks of colic as a newborn. The first time I walked the floor with her, I remember repeating the word *Jesus* hundreds of times as I paced, whispering His name, singing it, sometimes raising my voice above her crying. As I held Cindy close in my arms, I was acutely aware of bringing Jesus into that room with us. Prayer? Oh, yes! Inviting Jesus there with us—to comfort, calm, and relieve the pain.

It was our infant grandson, James, who missed his mummy and daddy so much when they went for a weekend of skiing, leaving him for the very first time. Not knowing his grandmother that much yet, he cried and cried. But it gave me a wonderful excuse to hold him close and walk the floor, whispering over and over in his ear a little 'bzzzz' sound that he seemed to love. But I also prayed and prayed while I walked, asking God to provide the security tiny James needed, security that only his parents could really give—security that I as his grandmother could not completely supply. And he settled down, experiencing at that early age God coming in answer to prayer to hold him closely in His supernatural arms.

As you've likely concluded, as a grandmother I snatch every opportunity to include God in my touching experiences with my grandchildren. Then they are not only touched by a caring human, but by the omnipotent God of heaven.

TRANSMITTED THROUGH PRAYER

Jesus was indignant when His disciples rebuked the people who were bringing children to Jesus to touch.

> And He took them in His arms, and began blessing them, and laying His hands on them (Mark 9:16).

In Guatemala busloads of women from the mountains who were brought to my meeting lined up to have me touch their little shiny-eyed babies. As I laid my hand on each one and prayed, the mothers were ecstatic. It was indeed one of the greatest privileges of my life, for I felt something of Jesus flowing through my hands to each of them.

Was Jesus including touching when He said to His followers (today's followers included), 'Truly, truly, I say to you, he who believes in Me, the works that I do shall he do also; and greater works than these shall he do; because I go to the Father' (John 14:12). Since touching was one of His most frequent 'works,' could He have been including what is transmitted in a touch? I do not see why not.

MARRIAGE TOUCHING

In our marriage, Chris and I have often said as we crawled into bed at night, 'This is the best time of the day.' Why? God knew when He ordained marriage that touching would produce the comfort, assurance, and drawing emotionally from each other so needed by weary mates at the end of a long day.

But the wee hours of the morning are my strongest

prayertimes. So as I lie next to Chris praying for him while he still sleeps at 3 or 4 o'clock, it is almost automatic to reach out and lay my hand on the top of his head. When I am communicating with the God of the universe about my husband, it seems so natural to touch Chris. Somehow there seems to be an adding of a physical dimension of God responding to that touching as He pours into Chris the things I am praying for.

A FATHER'S BLESSINGS

As a medical doctor, our son-in-law Skip knows the importance of touching. He also knows the importance of touching family members. But as the spiritual head of his house, he knows the importance of 'blessing touching.' For many years he has practised spiritual blessings in their home. Skip tells about it in his own words:

> As parents we are continually being encouraged in our efforts to nurture our children and spouses lovingly. God's Word and some recent writings on the importance of touching and blessing have had an impact on our family. Our spiritual and secular culture has been rather silent with respect to the importance of the blessing. Occasionally, we are affirmed by parents, teachers, and supervisors; however, touching is known to be vital in healthy social and emotional development.
>
> For several years we have shared together each week in personal blessings after our 'special' Sunday breakfast. Our children clamour (usually) to be the first blessed. Seated in our lap, the special person is surrounded by the rest and hugged and kissed by the 'blessor'. They are blessed in Jesus' name for general or specific requests. Other family members pipe in with particular things in that person they are thankful for and any special spiritual blessing they are led to offer. Frequently we ask for healing blessings. The filling of the sevenfold Spirit of the Lord is sometimes prayed. I like the blessing said about young Jesus, 'And Jesus increased in wisdom and stature, and in favour with God and men' (Luke 2:52, KJV). For my wife I am proud to

include blessings mentioned in Proverbs: 'Her children arise
and call her blessed; her husband also, and he praises her'
(31:28, KJV).

Recently Crista and Jenna were on my lap as we read
from an encyclopedia from 'chicken' to 'China.' Under the
word *child* we read that the five- to eight-year-old child is
actively forming his self-image based on interactions with
his parents and other children. By the pre-teen years more
of that approval begins to come from peers. As a family
encouraging and affirming one another with our words,
prayers, and affection, we covet God's cement to help us
grow together and strong in Him. The family blessing is one
of God's tools that helps us accomplish this.

Chris and I were there for one of those Sunday break-
fasts, and Skip moved on around the table to place his
hands on our heads when finished with his family. What an
awesome experience. And what an overwhelming family
prayertime! Jan told me that Jenna went to stay over Satur-
day night at the home of one of her girlfriends. Aghast, she
later told her parents that they didn't do anything on Sunday morning—'they just had breakfast.'

The first time I experienced hands blessing a child in
Skip and Jan's home was when they brought their firstborn,
Jenna, home from the hospital. Although she was less than
twenty-four hours old, no hospital could hold the child of
those two medical doctors. So Jan called ahead to see if I
would get things ready and carry the baby into the house.
'Jan, you've waited ten years for this child. Don't you want
to carry her over the threshold into your home yourself?'

'No,' she replied. 'We want you to carry the new baby
into the house and sit in the old green chair and pray for
her.' (The old green chair which had been my 'prayer
closet' for over twenty years—and now reupholstered and
in their living room.)

Well, I carried that newborn in and sat down in the old
green chair. But I couldn't sit there. I laid Jenna on the seat
and knelt beside her. As I laid my hands on that soft little
bundle and started to pray, I became aware of the new

mummy and daddy kneeling down on each side of me—
also laying their hands on their first offspring. *Praying!*

Our grandchildren have come in 'cousin pairs.' Cindy
had preceded her little cousin, Jenna, as our first grandchild
by just a month. And on my first time alone in their home
with our first grandchild, I had knelt beside her and prayed.
In the awesomeness of laying my hands on that new generation in our family, I had prayed fervently for God to put His
arms around her, to protect her, to guard her, and to
nurture her, and fill her with Himself. *God's hands touching her
with mine!*

TOUCHING HANDS

Jesus must have thought His hands in blessing had special
significance, for after a ministry of touching people of all
ages, He chose His hands in blessing as His final gesture
here on earth. When the risen Saviour left this earth, 'He
lifted up His hands and blessed them. And...while He was
blessing them, He parted from them' (Luke 24:50-51).

Hands always have been a vital part of blessings and
commissionings in Christianity. New missionaries, pastors,
and priests are sent into their calling from God with the
laying on of hands.

> At Antioch...while they were ministering to the Lord and
> fasting, the Holy Spirit said, 'Set apart for Me Barnabas and
> Saul for the work to which I have called them.' Then, when
> they had fasted and prayed *and laid their hands on them*, they
> sent them away (Acts 13:1-2, italics added).

The Bible certainly implies that something more than
symbolic happens when there is laying on of hands.

What they actually received through those hands we are
not told. And I used to wonder as I watched commissioning
services what, if anything, happened during the commissioning prayer. But now, as the recipient, I know there
is something from God. Whenever I go on an overseas trip,

launch a new facet of ministry, or begin a new year of my life, the board members lay hands on me.

I have been amazed at the difference in what I feel from different hands. Sometimes warmth, sometimes unexpected heat, and frequently something like electricity flowing to me. Friendly hugs from my board members are wonderful, but when prayer is added, God is not only involved, something *from Him* is transmitted.

Our family frequently has 'commissioning prayers' too, and not only for our newborn babies. The last time I left for India, Jan and Skip had a family prayertime for me around the old green chair at their own house. As I knelt, the entire family laid hands on me and one by one prayed for God to protect me, guide me, keep me safe. Again that spiritual something passed from them to me. We ended by hugging in a big entwined circle and wiping tears. *Family parting— including God*.

Our grandson Brett wasn't a month old yet when Jan was leaving him with me to go shopping. As she handed him to me, she asked, 'Where do you want to hold him?'

My immediate reply was, 'In the old green chair. Then I can do two things at once.' Jan paused a minute, sitting down across the room from us, savouring the scene.

As I held that tiny baby close, something just seemed to pour out from my being to him. 'Jan, I don't understand what happens when we touch like this, but it does.' When I was alone with him, tears trickled down my face as I felt this overwhelming 'grandma love' just flowing, even from the palms of my hands as they pressed on his little body. But it was when I began to pray that I included God's divine hands and arms touching that little boy. I don't understand 'touching,' but I certainly have experienced it—have been the recipient of its results.

MY MOTHER'S HANDS

Years ago whenever I was in a hospital bed or beside a little casket in the mortuary, or facing a crisis in our family, somehow Mother always managed to get the next plane to me. And her work-gnarled hand would soothe my brow or dry my tear-stained face. Through the years when I lost babies or my world fell apart, her warm, caring hand would automatically reach out to me. But there always was her praying that accompanied those precious hands.

As Mother got older, we frequently switched roles. After her husband of over twenty-five years (my stepfather) died, I was driving her home one night. I stopped the car on the roadside, and we talked deeply about her loneliness. Then I reached out my hand for hers and held it tightly as we prayed. I'll never know what she felt, but I can still vividly remember the electricity I felt go between our hands.

How often I would take her frail little body, racked with the physical infirmities of old age, into my arms. As I held that little lady close and prayed, I wonder what, if anything, she felt. Did she receive the power, the support, the caring, the love flowing from me—and from God as I prayed? She's in heaven now, so I'll have to wait to ask her.

As I get older and experience those not-so-spry and sometimes painful feelings, I know what I feel when my children hold me tight to their vital, powerful, youthful bodies. And when they add the dimension of prayer, God adds His vitality and power to our hug too.

Most humans, especially married couples, mothers and fathers, children and grandparents, know the importance of touching. But touching and praying adds another dimension—*God!*

CHAPTER EIGHT

When We Can't Touch, God Can

A T THE TIME I KNELT at the old green chair and my family prayed as I left for India in 1982, God also had given all four in Jan and Skip's family the same Bible verse for me:

> Have I not commanded you? Be strong and courageous! Do not tremble or be dismayed, for the Lord your God is with you *wherever* you go (Josh. 1:9, italics added).

There was a special need for this promise from God as I travelled that time in India. Political violence escalated day by day. Even in beautiful Bangalore they would not let me step out alone on the street until a car was waiting for me. Spreading government curfews made the planned seminar schedule touch and go, some being lifted just two hours before the start of our meeting. The morning I was to leave for Calcutta, news reports were ominous. As I read Joshua 1:9 once more, God emphasized just one word—*wherever!* God assured me, '*Wherever* you go, I will keep the promise they all prayed for you.' And I powerfully experienced

God's answers through His protection, power, and victory *wherever* I went all through that rigorous trip in India. God can reach us *wherever* we go!

WHEN YOU CAN'T TOUCH, MAKE A TRIANGLE

Our granddaughter Kathy was having trouble understanding spatial relations as we talked about her having to leave our family vacation at Lake Michigan and go home. So I assured her I would pray for her even if she was at home a thousand miles away.

'The great part about prayer is that it doesn't matter where you are, Kathy,' I assured her. 'You see, I just pray up to God in heaven for you; then God reaches into your heart wherever you are. It doesn't matter if you are in Minnesota or Washington or Michigan. I don't always know where you are, but God *always* knows exactly where you are.

'It's like making a triangle, Kathy. Put the palms of your hands together over your head, Honey. Now that's God at the tip of your fingers. And you and I each have an elbow. When you put your elbows together, that's when we are together like we are now on this vacation. But when you spread your elbows far apart, that's how we are sometimes when you have to go home. But we are still connected through God. So when I pray for you at my elbow, my prayer goes up that arm to God. Then God runs the prayer right down the other arm to you—no matter where you are.'

That made going home a lot easier for Kathy.

I learned to use this triangle when Chris had to leave for military duty in England as a B-17 bomber pilot in World War II. I never knew exactly where he was—on a mission, at the base, or in London for a few days. And I had no way of contacting him directly no matter how desperately I needed him. With every bomber raid over Germany, I did

not even know if he had returned to his base safely or had
been shot down and captured.

But as that young bride, I learned an important lesson:
*God could, and would, be there taking the cries of my heart directly to
Chris.* My heartcries for his protection, comfort, peace, and
even joy in the midst of battle were taken directly by God to
Chris' barracks or the cockpit of his plane. No, I could not
be there—but God could!

As I was typing this chapter, the phone rang and a weak
voice was calling for prayer—once more. The caller was a
wife and mother who has scleroderma, the fatal sickness
where the skin gradually turns stonelike. She had had to be
fed intravenously, but thanked us for praying, for now she
was able also to eat to some degree. Together we thanked
God for that miracle.

But then she told me about her concern for her ten-year-
old son who sometimes has a hard time handling his
mother's illness and hospitalization—and she feels so helpless. I assured her that one of the privileges of being in the
hospital was having lots of time to pray for her son; and,
although she could not reach him, God could—and
would—if she would pray. I explained the triangle of her
reaching up to God from her hospital bed and then God
reaching down to her son. I told her that she was not
helpless because her son desperately needed her to pray for
him. 'But I'm getting so weak,' she whispered. I assured her
that God understood, that just short sentence prayers
would do.

'Your prayers from your hospital bed may be the most
important thing you ever could do for your son,' I emphasized. 'They could turn around the whole direction of his
future life—much more than you could just by cooking,
doing laundry for him and being with him.' *Triangle prayers!*

WHEN WE CAN'T REACH TO TOUCH A FAMILY MEMBER, GOD CAN

Chris and I both have had to travel a lot in our ministries. No matter where our travels have taken us around the world, that triangle praying not only sends God with His answers to the other, but it somehow seems to connect us, too.

There is a deep loneliness when Chris and I must be apart from each other. And for at least thirty years I have prayed to God, 'O Lord, fill Chris with You in his loneliness—as I feel You filling me when I'm away from him.' And no matter whether I have been in Asia, Europe, Australia, or Africa, I have prayed, and God has reached out to wherever Chris has been—and filled the void in Chris' heart.

And when Chris had his cancer surgery, I could not be there every minute while he recovered. But he told me, as mentioned earlier, 'I could feel you praying. I felt like my body didn't even touch the bed. I was just upheld by a cradle of prayer.'

> Thy loving-kindness, O Lord, extends to the heavens, Thy faithfulness reaches to the skies (Ps. 36:5)

There is no limit to how far God can reach. And I am amazed at how God's arm can swivel at 360 degrees in that prayer triangle. When we pray to Him, it doesn't matter where on earth, or even in outer space, our family members may be, God's arm can find them.

WHEN WE CAN'T FIND LOVED ONES, GOD'S HAND CAN

There are times we don't even know where a family member is. No matter what time zone I'm in, I always carry a clock set on 'home time.' But, even so, I can't always keep track of where my family members are—or they where I am.

While I was flying home alone from Bombay, India, the political situation in the Middle East was very tense. My flight included air passage over those deserts in an Air India plane, and my husband was very concerned. Having been trained as a military pilot, he kept track of where my plane was by keeping in touch with the airlines information system. And he stayed up all night, not just worrying, but praying. Praying for his wife—somewhere out over those hostile deserts.

> If I take the wings of the dawn,
> If I dwell in the remotest part of the sea,
> Even there Thy hand will lead me,
> And Thy right hand will lay hold of me (Ps. 129:9-10).

Electronic communications and mail deliveries break down. While I was in India, it took me several hours and sometimes days to make phone contact with home while my mother-in-law was not expected to live. One of the greatest things about prayer is that the God who answers them is an *omnipresent* God. Even when no telephone or mail delivery is possible, there is One who still can and does transcend the miles across continents and oceans—*God*.

SO NEAR, YET SO FAR

The distance between you and your child's school, questionable social event, or just 'out with the gang' can be just as devastating as if there were an ocean in between. But God's hand can reach children in those places too.

The sting of those early family separations was greatly reduced for us by our praying for our children. We sent our little ones out into a cruel world—not alone but with God. At our 'front door praying' we prayed specifically about the bully on the playground, that day's difficult test, a tummy ache, or whatever was looming before them out there. Our hand could not hold theirs—and should not have. But we sent our children out with the invisible hand of God tightly holding theirs.

From the day our Jan entered school until our last child, Kurt, left high school, we never missed a day praying with each child at the door as he or she left, as mentioned in an earlier chapter. I'll admit there were times when our children were adolescents or teens that they rebelled at having to wait at the door. And sometimes the prayers had to be just a few words 'shot up to God on the run'. But, looking back, I know how important those prayertimes were—to them—and to us. They removed the fear and our possessiveness as God took over—when we couldn't. When we prayed for them, our children unknowingly had the same assurance as the psalmist in Psalm 73:23, 'Nevertheless I am continually with Thee [God]; *Thou hast taken hold of my right hand*' (italics added).

The first time I transported a little grandchild to her playschool, my daughter Jan warned, 'Don't forget to pray in the hall right inside the door there. She won't go in until you do!'

JUST A PRAYER APART

Although my mother and I experienced a lifetime of 'touching prayers' whenever we were together, the vast majority of our prayers were when we could not touch. And this is true of most family prayers. The percentage of times most family members can touch while praying is relatively small. As family members grow up, go to school, move away, or get married, physical touching can be spasmodic at best. So what do we do when we can't touch?

My mother had the answer for that too. Hundreds of times through the years she has reminded me, *'Remember, Evelyn, we're just a prayer apart.'* She said it with such finality—no questioning, no wavering. It was just a fact—an indisputable fact!

Living hundreds of miles from my mother in my adult life never broke our incredible closeness. How did we maintain that oneness? It was her quietly reaching for my hand and whispering to me every time we parted, 'We're just a prayer apart.' It became our shared secret after I married, then while I followed my husband in his military stint, our college and his studies and pastorates. In later years, the last phone call to Mother as I was leaving for overseas always would include, 'Remember, love, we're just a prayer apart!'—calming her motherly apprehension—and mine.

So, instead of distance separating my mother and me, our prayers have run like a triangle up to God and down to the other—the connection between us mysteriously, divinely unbroken.

When we can't touch our family member in need, God still can connect us. It was Jan's first night after extensive microsurgery in Mayo Clinic, and we could not be with her. In severe pain, she called my motel across the street in the middle of the night. 'Oh, Mother, it hurts so much; *please pray!*' What a struggle to be separated by so few blocks— and yet so completely—while I spent the rest of the night interceding to God for my child in her pain. The next morning as I walked into her hospital room, Jan smiled weakly and said, *'Thanks, Mother. Prayer is just like somebody holding your hand long distance.'*

AN ANCHOR AT HOME
It is extremely important for family members who are away to have an anchor back at home. They desperately need the security of the remaining family members, their caring about what has happened—and their unconditional love. They need a phone number or an address that will give them an anchor to hold on to—a place to direct their cries for help.

When families receive calls for help from those far away, a terrifying helplessness can set in. We want to run or fly to them immediately.—which is usually impossible. Panic can set in as parents and siblings wonder how to help. Or they even may dismiss the problem because they know there is nothing they can do about it anyway.

But how privileged is the distant family member whose

family back home *does* know what to do. Whose family knows that, even if they cannot go to their loved one, there is Somebody who *can*—God. How privileged if their families know how to *pray*.

It is not our caring or even our loving, as important as they are for the well-being of the absent family member, that will produce results in the difficult circumstances. Only God who can do that. And God reaches down to intervene in their need in response to our praying.

> The effectual, fervent *prayer* of a righteous person *avails much* (James 5:13, italics added).

Family SOS calls should elicit more than worry, panic, or even ignoring their plight. Fervent and persistent prayer by the family at home should explode spontaneously.

TELEPHONE PRAYER CONNECTION

Our family has kept the long distance phone lines busy since our first child went away to college. We have felt those phone bills were one of the greatest investments we ever could make in our children. Urgent calls of 'Please pray—quick!' or 'Mother, call the prayer chain' are familiar sounds in our house. Even ordinary calls almost always end up with a promise to pray or a silent resolve to multiply and intensify our praying for them.

When Kurt and Margie were living in New York, they helped prevent an abortion in a young girl by taking her into their home. But they were unprepared for her lifestyle. 'Mother, how do you answer when we tell her driving with a gang of teenagers and throwing bottles through car windows isn't right—and she, startled, asks us what *we* do for fun? Please pray, Mother.'

As members live away from family, situations frequently arise which they can't handle alone. But they don't have to handle them alone. A phone call or letter to a praying Christian family back home sends the prayer up to God;

and, although the family can't help in person, God can—
and does. In answer to those prayers!

Just as I was writing about an anchor at home, our
phone rang. It was our daughter-in-love Margie, now herself pregnant again. 'Kurt had stomach flu all night and
can't team teach with me in Sunday School this morning.
Please pray!' Then she continued, 'And I feel so empty this
week—with James so sick and me still not feeling well after
our bouts of stomach flu. Worse yet, Kurt wrote today's
lesson, and he was going to lead today. I have his notes, but
have only fifteen minutes to get it together.'

My heart reached out to her. 'Margie,' I replied, 'it is in
your weakness, like Paul's, that the power of Christ will rest
upon you. I know—it is the story of my life and always has
been true for me. Don't worry about what you will say. You
have lived that Sunday School lesson for many years. So
just let the Holy Spirit recall the answers to their questions
from what God has done for you. I *know* He will!'

While Margie was teaching, I spent much of the time
praying to God for an outpouring of His power, not only on
her, but on the whole class. One of the greatest privileges of
my life has been to have my children feel they have an
anchor at home where they can call for prayer—any time
or under any circumstance.

AN ANCHOR FOR DAN AND NANCY

Of all the prayers phoned to our home, by far the most
frequent were from our Nancy during Dan's three-and-
a-half years of that job disaster. Living a thousand miles
away afforded only brief and scattered visits, but the prayer
link never broke. My mother's 'We're just a prayer apart'
became a way of life for this mother and daughter too.
Sometimes I almost think we are much closer *because* she is
so far away.

Their needs were endless—and the urgent requests
almost continual. Day after day huge mountains loomed
before them—from selection of a lawyer, to working with

Senator Grassley's office, to appearing before the National Merit Board. They needed prayer!

Then Nancy phoned for prayer because little Kathy had fallen down the stairs and broken her leg. Nancy was getting another degree by extension with constant roadblocks. Cindy's needed surgery was postponed because they found she had a bleeding problem. And on and on the SOS phone calls came home. And over and over we prayed.

You'll recall that phoning prayer requests all started in Rockford back in 1968 when our 'What Happens When Women Pray' ladies experimented with using the telephone to communicate the prayer needs resulting in 'telephone prayer chains'. But it was the call-backs with the answers that convinced them, without my knowing it, that God really does answer when we communicate by phone—if we really take time to pray.

IN NANCY'S OWN WORDS

Here in her own words Nancy tells how much prayer has meant to her:

> Many families separated by miles keep in touch by phone or letters. Unfortunately, many of those communications deteriorate from informational to indifference or even gossip.
>
> I grew up understanding that God is a part of everyday activities and decisions. And whenever I call home, the conversation closes with, 'We'll pray about that'—and they do. It does not necessarily need to be a crisis. Including God through prayer in the day-to-day activities of marriage, jobs, and raising children keeps our family not only well informed—but close.
>
> Whenever we share, unload, or even pray with a friend or a counsellor, it can be very beneficial. But when we unload or share with a family member, there is an added dimension. The depth and permanence of family love is different. And it creates intensely personal and caring prayers. And that is what I have experienced every time I have called home through these many years.

WHEN THEY PRAY FOR US, GOD'S ARM REACHES US

One of the most important gifts I ever received was a gold cross on a chain. Chris gave it to me when I first started travelling alone extensively. The card read, 'Remember when you are out there alone, there is somebody at home loving you and praying for you.' How often when things got difficult I would reach up, hold on to that little cross, and feel the assurance of those prayers of my husband.

When I went to Seoul, Korea to teach at the International Prayer Assembly in 1984, Chris gave me a letter to carry always, saying, 'I have two reasons to write this letter. First it is my hope that as you carry it, it will be a constant reminder of *my prayers for you*. Prayer that gives a sense of His power, His presence, and His ability to meet every need you will have. He is able. Second, to be a reminder of how much I love you and anxiously await the day of your return.'

The prayers from Dan and Nancy have also flowed this way to me. I too share my many needs with them, not just pray for them. When I first asked little Nancy at our 'front door prayertime' over thirty years ago to pray for me because Mother had a problem that day, it has borne much fruit. I cherish the freedom to ask for their prayers in my ministry, in my personal life, on boards where I serve, and my relationships. I'm anxious to get to heaven and see all of their prayers stored up in golden bowls up there.

I have had the same kinship in prayer with Kurt through the years and now also his Margie. There is no feeling of superiority or authority over them in our spiritual life together. No, I eagerly admit my needs to them also— coveting their prayers for their mother. It is the 'bearing of one another's burdens' of Galatians 6:2 in action in this open and sweet family relationship.

As I have mentioned in this book so often, the prayer support from Jan and Skip has been so wonderful. Many times, in the depth of despair, inadequacy for a task or lack of wisdom, I have poured out my heart to them. And they have fervently and faithfully wrestled at the Throne of Grace for me. Jan and son-in-love Skip have been some of my strongest prayer supporters through the years—at home and around the world.

When overseas, I always rotate the phone calls home among my husband and three children's families. Once in Aberdeen, Scotland, I felt strong spiritual warfare during the committee prayertime the night before my seminar. I phoned Jan and Skip, whose turn it was to get the call— this time for prayer. Jan's reply to me was, 'This is for you, Mother, from Romans 8:37: *"more than conquerers!"* ' (AV, italics added) As I read it again at 6 o'clock the next morning, there was a rush of tears—of relief, of complete trust in Jesus, of victory to come. And it did come.

When I returned from my Taiwan prayer seminar tour and the wonderful power of God we experienced, Jan told me that every day while I was gone she had prayed that only God would be seen, and only He would be glorified. And that prayer was answered.

Jan's prayers for overseas trips have often been written to me in notes. My first overseas ministering took me alone to Australia in 1980. I wiped tears from time to time all the way to Australia with her note telling me that every day while I was gone she and Skip would kneel at the old green chair—and pray for me. And Skip's precious notes always are the Scriptures God has given him for me while I am gone.

And her note as I left for South Africa, a country torn by racial terrorism at that time, emphasized that she was praying about my *reason* for going from Luke 24:45-50: 'That repentance for forgiveness of sins should be proclaimed in His name to all the nations.' God answered that prayer throughout the whole strife-torn trip.

But I don't have to be overseas to receive prayer notes from my family. While I was writing my *Battling the Prince of Darkness* book, I was frequently tempted to soft-pedal some of the harsh biblical truths about Satan and hell. But it was a note from Jan only two miles away that I kept taped by my computer desk the whole time I wrote that book that gave me that godly boldness. It was part of the spiritual armour section from Ephesians 6:19-20 where Paul asked prayer for himself from those wearing the armour of God:

> And pray for me also, that whenever I open my mouth, words may be given me so that I will fearlessly make known the mystery of the Gospel for which I am an ambassador in chains. Pray that I may declare it fearlessly, as I should (NIV).

PRAYER FOR BOLDNESS!

Also I am deeply indebted to my sister and brother-in-law, Maxine and Rudy, who pray faithfully for me every day while I travel. When they were in the Philippines for a two-year missions stint, we kept their picture on our refrigerator and prayed for them every day. But I was overwhelmed when they told me how much they prayed for me on my last trip to India. As members of my Twenty-Four-Hour Prayer Clock, they set their alarm and *got up two hours early every day to pray for me and my ministry there*. Having travelled extensively around the world, they understood the dangers and needs I would have.

Also Maxine went to her Bible every day and wrote down and dated what God had given her to pray for me as she followed my itinerary. Just a few are:

> Send angels ahead of her to prepare the way (Ex. 23:20)...
> In Calcutta, that vast city needing Christ—power is in God's hands...
> 'Not by might, nor by power but by My Spirit says the Lord' (Zech. 4:6)...
> Isaiah 40:31 in that hot climate in Bombay...
> 'The angel of the Lord encamps around those who fear Him' (Ps. 34:7)...
> Romans 16:20—that God would crush Satan—for her and Operation Mobilization leaders...

That, like Stephen from Acts 6:8, she would be God's
woman full of grace and power...
And on the way home, that He protects the way of His
faithful ones— from Proverbs 2:8.

When my mother died there was a deep loss in my life.
My ministry calendar, phone calls, and letters always
prompted not only her motherly concern but her deep
prayer for me. But now I no longer can shoot an SOS to her
for prayer. But God has laid on other hearts my mother's
mantle of prayer. I have a deep and rare treasure in my
family's prayer for me.

WHEN THEY WON'T TOUCH
There are times when family members deliberately cut off
touching. A child runs away or a spouse disappears. Also
there are times when family members could touch, but are
emotionally separated and refuse to communicate. Perhaps
they have distanced themselves from the family deliberately
because of sin, rebellion, aloofness, an independent lifestyle,
or an unforgiving spirit. Our arms ache to hold that dear
one close to us—as in years past, but he or she will not
allow it.

I recall being told once when longing to feel the healing
of a hug from an estranged extended-family member, 'The
last thing she wants you to do is hug her!'

This is a sign loved ones need their space—but also is a
sign they need prayer more than ever. At those times, there
is just the standing by, keeping heart and door open to
them—interceding. It is a time to hang on without wavering to God's desire and ability to bridge the gap that
separates loved ones. It is a time of deep, earnest, persistent
prayer—sometimes day and night.

There is no distance too great, and there is no rift too
wide, to stop prayer.

CHAPTER NINE

'Releasing' Prayers

V ERY EARLY ON NEW YEAR'S morning of 1990 I was lying in bed praying for each child, grandchild, and my husband, not only for a new year but a new decade. I prayed for each one individually—for specific needs and then for God to fill each with Himself. Then an overwhelming feeling swept over me that I should *release* my whole family to God.

I bundled them all up in a package in my mind and gave them to God—for His complete will. 'Lord, do anything You need to them to make them what You want them to be. Lord, I release them all to You for whatever You know is best for them—because I know You never make a mistake. Lord, You know every facet and step of the future of each one of them, and You never make a mistake!'

As I picked up a section of our newspaper, my eyes fell on the picture of the first TV newscaster of our area whom we watched every night in the 1940s. Dead. Same age as my husband, Chris. A little apprehension crept into my heart as I wondered, am I releasing Chris for *that* reason? Then I cried out to the Lord, 'But *he* is Yours too Lord! And *me* too! I can't release everybody *else* and not myself.'

There had been many times before, and have been since, that God has required me to pray releasing a family member to Him for His will—not mine. Just one releasing prayer never has done it. Whenever a new difficult decision has arisen, the releasing prayer has had to be prayed again—and again—and again.

But these are not easy prayers to pray. We all feel that somehow we own our human possessions—the one we married, the ones to whom we gave birth, our parents, our grandparents. It is very difficult to give up those we call 'family' to the will of another—even if it is God's.

RELEASED NOT TO ANYBODY—BUT TO GOD

Later that year while going through an extended family crisis (which included some family members I had released that New Year's morning), God spoke so powerfully to me out of 2 Timothy:

> For this reason I also suffer these things, but I am not ashamed; for I know *whom* I have believed and am convinced that He is able to guard what I have entrusted to Him until that day (2:12, italics added).

I sank to my knees by my prayer pouf and cried, 'Lord, I have completely committed my husband, each child, each grandchild, my service, my will, my body, my health, and my strength to You many times. Now that I'm going through this crisis, I know You *will* keep and guard it all— until that day!'

Released—not to just *anybody*—but to God! I know in *Whom (deity)* not in *whom* (human) I have believed. This is not releasing my family members into the hands of a human leader of a different religion, a human counsellor, a peer group with a different set of moral and social values, or a different human mentor to guide them. No, this is releasing them to the omniscient God of the universe! He knows the end from the beginning, knows all the 'whys' and 'what ifs' of our lives. He alone is capable—and worthy—to have us entrust our human possessions to Him.

> Oh, the depth of the riches both of the wisdom and know-ledge of God! How unsearchable are His judgments and unfathomable His ways! (Rom. 11:33)

GOD'S SIDE OF OUR RELEASING

How relieved God must be when we release someone we love for His will. Relieved that He no longer has to wrestle with us as we try to hinder His perfect will in the life of that family member. Relieved that the roadblocks to His dealing with our loved ones we keep throwing up in front of Him finally are removed—and we at last have trusted Him enough not to fight against what He knows is best.

Of course, God is sovereign. And He frequently bypasses us to accomplish His will in a loved one. But in tenaciously holding on to a family member for our will in them, we create a struggle between His will and ours. A battle between divine will and human will.

When teaching how to pray in the Lord's Prayer, Jesus made it very clear that we are to release our wills to the *Father's* will.

> Our Father who art in heaven,
> Hallowed be Thy name.
> Thy kingdom come.
> *Thy* will be done,
> On earth as it is in heaven (Matt. 6:9-10, italics added).

When there was a struggle of wills in heaven as Lucifer (Satan) wanted to be like God, he was violently thrown from heaven. But God deals more kindly with His children on earth. He just expects us to *want* His will—and then to release all our human possessions *for* His will. Then His perfect will can be done in our family on earth—just like it is now in all of heaven.

A woman named Betty called from Texas in late 1990 saying, 'I'm beside myself because my two soldier sons are en route to Desert Storm in Saudi Arabia and my daughter-in-law is already there.' Together on the phone we prayed, releasing them into God's hands, and then thanking Him for whatever His will would be in their lives. Feeling God's incredible peace, Betty thanked me and hung up. Shortly after that a close friend called me and mentioned that when her son in the armed forces in Saudi Arabia was unable to get a Bible to read and to worship God, he began examining his relationship with Jesus—and for the first time accepted Him as the Saviour and Lord of his life. *God's will!*

Releasing frees God to flow unhindered into our family members' lives. Frees Him to reprove and prune instead of our playing God and trying to protect our family members from anything hard. Releasing frees God to call them into His service instead of our wanting our children to be wealthy and succeed by the world's standards. Frees God to open those fabulous doors of ministry we have been trying to hold shut by our stubborn wills.

CAREER RELEASING

God gives each of our children talents and abilities, and it seems so natural for parents to want our children to use them to succeed in life, to become financially secure and to have the comforts that perhaps they missed. But releasing our children to use those talents for God's will, whatever that might entail, is not always easy.

I could relate the series of releasing prayers for the education and career of each of our children, but some of my releasing prayers for Kurt will reflect what was prayed for each of them.

Our praying God's will for Kurt's future started at his birth, but especially came into focus for him at his high school college entrance tests. 'Call the prayer chain,

Mother. Tomorrow are my SAT tests,' he nervously ordered. When I answered that I had already called and asked them to pray for God's will concerning how he would do the next day, Kurt put his hands on his hips and exclaimed, 'Oh, boy. It'll be just my luck that it is God's will that I flunk!'

Then I explained to him that God, knowing his talents and aptitudes, would open and close doors accordingly. 'And God's closed doors may be more important than the open ones, for God knows what is best for you, Kurt.'

He did pass, and his reason for wanting to attend Bethel College written in his application brought a thrill to my heart: 'I grew up in a church-oriented environment. I accepted Christ as a small child and have recently reaffirmed the decision. I believe that God's will is the most important thing in my life, and going to Bethel is in His will.'

Then it was during his entrance tests for his doctoral studies in physics that I, not he, struggled so hard with God's will, as I told you about earlier. As I prayed those three hours on two consecutive nights while he took those tests, much of the praying time was about my willingness for God's will in Kurt's career. With deep tearful praying, at 8:20 the first night I emptied myself of every desire I had for Kurt. I released him for God's will, not mine. Then my prayertime turned to worshipping God for who He is in my son's life! The God who knew what talents He put in Kurt at conception—and thus what his career should be!

But when the doctoral training was over, more questions of God's will emerged. As Kurt worked on his first place of employment, I had put an SOS on the telephone prayer chain: 'Pray for Kurt that he will know God's *exact* open door for him.' Then I had one of the most precious moments I ever have had with my son. As we knelt together at my prayer pouf, Kurt squeezed my hand and put his head next to mine as we wrestled with God—once again giving him over to God for *God's* open door.

Kurt was struggling with finishing his doctoral thesis and getting interviews in areas where he wanted to live. One Monday morning Margie, Kurt, and I sat clumped together by the kitchen table, holding hands and praying, 'Only Your will, God!'

As he was leaving to give a presentation to a prospective company, Kurt stopped and prayed, 'O God, put me where I will be the *most worth to You*. Father, as I go to give this presentation, make me what You want me to be. Lord, if my pride needs them to rub my face in the dirt by their reactions, O Lord, You know I don't want that to happen, but if You know I need that kind of response, OK, Lord.'

Kurt's questions were the usual ones through the tedious months of finding God's will. 'How can I wait that long, Mother?' 'How can I really know what His will is?' And finally, exasperated, he looked at me and said seriously, 'Why doesn't God just write it in the sky, Mother?'

During all of this, Kurt and Margie went to the Inter-Varsity Christian Fellowship Urbana Missions Conference because they were struggling with whether or not it was God's will for them to go to China and share Jesus through their much-needed professions as teachers or to stay in America. They had prayed, but now their praying for God's will escalated. And I prayed continually while they were there, 'Lord, keep them from being swayed emotionally in a way You do not want and are not calling.' Then, 'Lord, lead them to exactly the person or people You want them to talk with. Don't let them miss it if You are calling them to foreign missions. *God, only Your will. No more, no less!*'

Returning from Urbana where several mission executives eagerly had told Kurt and Margie there definitely were openings for them in China teaching English and physics, they prayed and prayed. Then we knelt by the prayer pouf, and I had the deep privilege of praying with and for them once again, 'O God, if it is Your will, don't let them miss it. But don't let them go if it is not Your number one will. Don't let them get ahead of Your timing. Prepare them as much and as long as You know is needed.' Both Kurt and Margie—after years of urgings of some kind from God to go perhaps to China—were submitting to God to go—or not to go—now or later.

And there was Kurt's wanting to be part of my ministry for years, and now adding Margie, who felt the same. As the three of us sat holding hands on our sofa, we dreamed and chatted about it—and then gave it to God for His will. Kurt just added as I write this, 'Even today, the story is not finished. My first position was temporary and far from both families. Looking back, we understand that God knew I had been "Harold's son" and then "Evelyn's son" for too long. I needed to follow God through *personal* commitment, not Christian peer pressure.'

Parents are tempted to pray for an immediate big salary, important connections in business, and overnight success; but giving up what in our hearts we want them to do is different. However, our omniscient God knows the outcome of each move in our children's lives—and, if we let Him, will direct in the way only He knows best for them. Our family verse, Romans 8:28, says that God will work out everything for good to those who love Him—only if they are called according to *His* purpose—not the parents' wills.

Marked in my Bible is my prayer for my family members (like Epaphras' prayer): 'Always labouring earnestly for you in his prayers, *that you may stand perfect and fully assured in all the will of God*' (Col. 4:12).

JAN'S RELEASING—IN HER OWN WORDS

I asked Jan to describe her releasing prayer experience. It follows:

> When, after years of our trying to conceive, God sent us the baby that was to become our Jenna, there are no words to describe our joy. Many times before her birth I thanked God for the privilege of carrying that baby. Then one day it happened. God said, 'I want her back.'
>
> 'What do You mean, You want her back! After all this

waiting and surgery, You want me to give her up?' As the depths of my emotions rolled, I heard the still small voice again, 'I want her back.'

Then I understood. I had to release this baby back to God *for His purposes*. Then I found myself playing a little game. My mind said, 'If I give God the baby, then He'll let me keep it.' But another part of my brain said, 'You foolish one! Do you think God is so stupid He can't see through that?' *I reasoned that if I intended to do what God was asking, I was going to have to do it, knowing that God might take me up on my promise—and that I could accept it if He did.*

The prayer became a lot harder to pray at that point. I knew I had to pray it and that I would pray it, but it still took several days before I was able to say: 'God, this child is Yours. If she will never know You (through salvation), and if she is as close to You now as she will ever be, then take her now, before she is born.'

It was the hardest prayer I had ever prayed. But I meant it—even if He took me up on it. Since her birth, I have had to give Jenna back on different issues many times since then, but these have been small in comparison, and I keep reminding myself of *whose child she really is*.

In regard to another releasing experience, Jan recalls:

Several years later Mother was preparing to go to South Africa. This was during the peak of their civil unrest. During my mother's preparation, we talked about martyrs and what God had in store for them—and how she had asked God years before for the privilege of being one for Him (see Rev. 6:9-11). Shortly after, I was awakened in the middle of the night by God. 'I want you to release your mother to be a martyr.' Now, it's one thing to release someone who's sitting home making cookies, and quite another to release someone who is to go speak in a volatile atmosphere to racially mixed audiences about forgiveness. To give her up to go overseas, OK. Maybe even to die. But to give her up to be tortured? God, how could You ask me for that? Then His still small answer came. 'For My glory.'

After hours of struggling and weeping, it was finally OK. 'All right, God, if You want to take her; if my kids lose their grandmother, even if she's tortured for Your sake, I accept your will.' *And I knew from my previous experience that when I said it, I had to mean it—because He might take me up on it.*

RELEASING PRAYERS: NOT AN INSURANCE POLICY

Jan and I have talked much about whether God, when He tests us, *just wants us to be willing* to give loved ones up like Abraham and his son Isaac—or whether He really *will take us up on our releasing prayers.* God had said to Abraham in Genesis 22:2, 'Take now your son, your only son, whom you love, Isaac, and...offer him there [on a Moriah mountain] as a burnt offering.' And Abraham, with his heart breaking, had obeyed God right up through binding Issaac, laying him on the altar, and lifting the knife to slay him. (A missionary to Taiwan, Jeanne Swanson, told me to try inserting my own child's name in the place of Isaac.) But then the angel of the Lord called to Abraham from heaven telling him not to slay his son, 'for now I know that you fear [reverence] God, since you have not withheld your son' (Gen. 22:13). And then God miraculously provided the ram for the sacrifice. *All God wanted was for Abraham to be willing!*

God has not taken any of the loved ones Jan gave Him either. But this one biblical example is not necessarily what God will do in every instance of releasing a loved one to His will. When God tests us as He did Abraham, He isn't under any obligation to say, 'Now that you have obeyed and released your possession to My will, I will let you have your will.'

'Mother,' Jan warned, 'it is important to realize that just because we release someone or something to God for His will, it does not mean He will do things as *we* want. *Releasing is not an insurance policy!*'

THE BLESSING OF OBEYING AND RELEASING

In the Abraham-Isaac story, the angel called to Abraham a second time from heaven and gave him God's *reward* for being willing. '*Because* you have done this thing, and have not withheld your son, your only son [declares the Lord], indeed I will greatly bless you...and in your seed all the nations of the earth shall be blessed, *because* you have obeyed My voice' (Gen. 22:16-18, italics added).

When we have released our family members to God, He has poured out His blessings on us too. We have had a new appreciation of each family member's preciousness to us and to God, producing so much sweeter relationships within our family. Thankfulness for each member is so much stronger.

And in releasing prayers, a new realization that they are His, not ours, emerges. As Jan puts it, 'Releasing authority and control over your loved ones is liberating because when you release *them, you* are released from the responsibility and worry over what happens to them.' Not that it removes our stewardship in taking care of them or our being concerned for them or our intercessory praying for them. No, those are multiplied after we release them to God. *But it is that they are now in the hands of the all-loving, all-powerful God of heaven—who has owned them all along!*

RELEASING REQUIRES FAITH IN WHO GOD IS

But being able to release our loved ones through prayer to God's will and not our own requires an unshakable faith in who God is.

You'll recall earlier mention of Jan's going to Mayo Clinic for microsurgery to correct a problem that had kept her from conceiving a child. Skip and Jan had given the matter of having a baby to God for His will for ten years. The night before Jan was to leave for Mayo, several of us met to pray with her. Kneeling, with all of us laying our hands on her, Jan trembled as she wept and struggled, and again gave the matter of her having a baby to God. But what she said as she stood up showed what she really thought of God. 'Oh, Mother,' she sobbed as we hugged tightly and wept together, 'if God doesn't have a baby for me, I *know* He has something better!'

My hardest prayer while Jan knelt was releasing my privilege of being a grandmother. But I did. And my response through my tears to her was, 'Oh, Jan, if God doesn't give you this baby, maybe now that you are a medical doctor He has a million little babies somewhere He wants you to hold in your arms.'

WHEN GOD DOES TAKE US UP ON A RELEASING PRAYER—FROM MARGIE

At my request, my daughter-in-love Margie wrote the following tender releasing incident from her own family:

> When your hand is clenched tightly around that which you love, it is no easy thing to open that hand and watch the object of your affection fly away. Especially when that object is your child—not holding merely your affection, but all your time, talents, sweat, tears, and your very life invested in a beautiful person you call your child.
>
> Releasing a child, I believe, is one of earth's most difficult trials. That is why God asked Abraham to give up Isaac. And the very God of heaven Himself was willing to be our example, for Romans 8:32 tells us, 'He [God]...did not spare His own Son, but gave Him up for us all.'
>
> I was thirteen when I watched my parents release my older brother, Bob. He was a very bright boy and popular in school. Baseball and football were exciting to him, and he received the all-school sportsmanship award. He and Dad played together on summer teams, and they were as close as any father and son combination I ever have seen. Bob was a serious Christian all through high school, and the coaches and classmates could tell the difference Jesus made in his life.
>
> When Bob graduated from high school, he started his

own business at age eighteen, aligning himself with the local Caterpillar Tractor company. Life was very good.

I remember the day Bob came home from college registration with new textbooks in hand. The future looked bright, but he had suffered some feverishness earlier in the summer. His doctors were stumped and blamed it on stress. Later doctors diagnosed the illness as histoplasmosis, a fungal disease of the lungs that later attacked Bob's brain. He never made it to his first day of college classes.

The next two years were filled with trips to the hospital, the last six months driving four hours each way to a larger metropolitan medical centre. My dad, having to work, travelled every weekend to see Mom and Bob. Every day Mom saw her son become worse and go through one nightmarish medical test after another. All this time our parents and we three girls gathered spontaneously to pray. Occasionally, we would pick a day to fast together and pray for Bob—even our eleven-year-old sister joined us. It was these prayertimes and the prayers of our close extended family plus the unsolicited prayers of hundreds of Christians that got us through.

After two years of hospitals, Bob came home, the doctors hoping he might recover somewhat. The healthy football player was a weak man in a wheelchair, unable even to feed himself. I saw the muscles in my mother's arms grow big from lifting her son. Yet who could give up hope?

As Mom struggled through each day, she was praying, 'God, not my will but Yours.' Dad, however, couldn't pray that way of releasing Bob. He felt praying God's will showed lack of faith or weakness. 'Wasn't that giving up hope?' he would ask.

My older sister, Vicki, was being prepared by God first, coming alone to the place of releasing Bob two weeks before Mom and Dad could. Finally, as the burden of Bob's sickness grew greater on the family and on Bob, my dad and mom agreed on a very, very difficult decision. Together they must take Bob to Isaac's altar. They must go to Abraham's 'distant place alone' (Gen. 22:4). They must unclench their hands and see the work of God. Finally, they could pray together, 'Father, Thy will be done.' One week later Bob died in his sleep. Two years of struggle were over.

Releasing—giving God everything—praying 'not My will but Thine' permeated all of Jesus' life. Can we do any less?

RELEASING PRAYERS: NOT A DEATH CERTIFICATE

Releasing does not cause death, but it does prepare *us* for that loved one's homegoing. A woman came to me a while after she had attended my prayer seminar. 'Did I kill my father? Did I kill my father?' she cried. 'My father had been in prison for many years when I released him to God for His will in your seminar. Weeks later I received notification that my father had died in prison and, because they had lost his records, I had not been notified. When I checked the date of his death,' she sobbed, 'it was the same day I released him! Did I kill him?'

'No, you did not cause his death,' I assured her. The releasing just prepared *you* for his death.'

When we release a loved one to God for His will, it is we, not the loved one who are prepared for the inevitable death. We don't kill loved ones.

Although I didn't release my miscarriages and stillborn baby to God until after I had gone through the agony of losing them, our Judy was different. Afflicted with spina bifida, she lived paralyzed from the waist down for seven months, and after months our doctor told us to take her directly to the hospital from his office—because she could not live.

That night, in the blackness of my bedroom in Stanchfield, I agonized in prayer on my knees until dawn. I fought and struggled until finally I could release her to God's will—not mine. Until I could release her *for Him to have*—not for Chris and me to have. But I did not kill her by being able at last to give her to God for His will. No, it only prepared me to give her up. And two months later they placed her in that little coffin. The grieving was there, but not the battle. I had released Judy into God's loving arms.

FAMILY POWER STRUGGLES

In all families there are conscious, or at least subconscious, power struggles. Toddlers fight to assert their personhood. Primary school children vie with their parents for control while being model pupils at school. Primary children try to substitute peer acceptance for family. Adolescents fight to discover who they are in the family pecking order. Teenagers struggle for independence from the whole family. Mates try to dominate their spouse's time and attention. Wives struggle to become the women God created them to be in a male-dominated society. Husbands try to hold on to their authority over other family members as they go through these various stages. So, how do we resolve this age-old power struggle in families?

Although it may not be easy, there is a simple prayer we can pray that will break the family power struggle: every family member releasing in prayer every other member to God's will—not their own.

RELEASING MYSELF

The hardest prayers for me to pray are those when I must decide between family and God. My heart at times seems powerfully pulled in two directions—God and family.

My life's goal has been to be conformed to the image of God's Son Jesus (Rom. 8:29). And it was said of Him in Hebrews 10:7, 'Then I said, "Behold, I have come to do Thy will, O God." ' This too is my only purpose for living—to do God's will. I have given myself to be a handmaid of the Lord, meaning I am one who has given her will, not just her lifestyle, to the Lord.

God specifically started calling me to win the lost in the world to Jesus in 1980, and from then on has repeatedly called. I was completely broken when God called me again to Jesus' words from Luke 15:4 to forget the ninety-nine and go find the lost sheep. I cried, 'O God, take me where *You* want me!' Since going meant leaving my two brand new grandchildren, I sobbed and prayed, 'Lord, exchange my empty arms for one sinner finding Jesus in India. No, Lord, many!' And just last year at our 'Lord, Change Me' board retreat, I cried to God, 'No matter *what the cost*, I will finish what You gave me to do—win the lost!' And that is when the joyous rewards from God come:

> And everyone who has left houses or brothers or sisters or father or mother or children or farms for My name's sake shall receive many times as much, and shall inherit eternal life (Matt. 19:29).

I have struggled deeply with how I handle what Jesus said clearly to me in Matthew 10:37:

> He who loves father or mother more than Me is not worthy of Me; and he who loves son or daughter more than Me is not worthy of Me.

But the answer is in Jesus' word *more*. It is my priorities—and balance.

Doing God's will includes all facets of my life—ministry and family. Balancing the two according to God's perfect will is imperative, but not always easy. Keeping my priorities the same as God's priorities for me takes constant evaluating and committing them over again to God.

I get great joy in serving my family, as I'm sure God wants me to. I am completely happy when surrounded by my entire family, giving myself wholeheartedly to them. However, there have been these deep, deep calls from God and my repeatedly releasing myself to His will. And I have wept before God trying to discern His sovereign balance. But the secret is in the releasing of both my family and myself to God's will.

GOD'S CHOICE, NOT MINE

My husband left his first pastorate after only three-and-a-half years. I had at last got curtains to fit that whole new parsonage, and when we moved into our colonial style house in Rockford, none of the curtains fitted! I had torn myself away from all the people I had learned to love deeply in that first pastorate, and I cringed at going through that every three years! *But I knew in my heart the choice was not mine—nor Chris'. It was God's.* Before that first move I had prayed and prayed about every church where Chris had candidated, and felt God had shown me which one was His choice. But I firmly held on to my belief that God had to tell *Chris* where He wanted him as a young pastor to serve Him—not *me*. I was to submit to God's will—and release Chris to follow it.

During the next move from Rockford after fourteen-and-a-half years it was even harder for me to release my husband, because he was leaving the pastorate and going to work and teach at Bethel College and Seminary. We were at the height of our 'What Happens When Women Pray' project in that church, and I wondered if God, for the first time, was making a mistake. It certainly seemed so to me. But my releasing it for God's will—not mine—came. And then I watched as God, who hadn't made a mistake, opened doors beyond anything I ever could have planned or chosen for us in the new place of service.

Although there have been times I have struggled to put in practice my deep belief about releasing, God has given me the grace and strength to live that way with every member of my family.

MY HUSBAND'S RELEASING PRAYER

While I was holding seminars in Japan, a secular newspaper reporter in Tokyo, mirroring his country's male-dominated society, asked me during an interview, 'How does your husband cope with you being the teacher and speaker?'

Nodding at Chris in another part of the room, I answered, 'He's sitting right over there. Why don't you ask him for yourself?'

I was startled and thrilled at my husband's profound

answer. Here, in Chris' own words, is what he told that reporter:

'I believe the Christian husband is the spiritual head of his household, God having entrusted him with his wife and children's physical and spiritual care. The Bible says that those to whom something has been entrusted are stewards; thus the husband and father is the steward of the wife and children whom God has entrusted to him. So that also makes him the steward of his wife's and children's gifts and talents from God. As a steward he is *responsible* not only to free them to use their talents from God, he also must encourage and assist them to do so. Also, as the steward of these family members, the husband *will give an account to God* as to whether he has hindered or helped them in the use of their God-given talents.'

> It is required of stewards that one be found trustworthy (1 Cor. 4:2).

Here are Chris' expanded beliefs about husbands as stewards: 'There is a great tragedy occurring in Christian America. Somehow we have come to believe that only men can exercise the God-given talents that He has provided for His children. There is no scriptural basis for only part of God's children receiving and using gifts and talents from God. And if God has entrusted a talent or gift to a household member, then everything about that home ought to encourage it. If not, the steward has failed in his responsibility and falls in the category of Jesus' unfaithful, wicked, slothful servant. (See Matt. 25:26 and Luke 19:22.)

'I'm often asked how I feel about a wife whom God is using outside the home. Shouldn't I be carrying on the ministry that she is—instead of her? Perhaps so, except for one thing—it was she who was called and gifted by God to minister as she does. I didn't decide this—God did. My place, and my joy, is to act as best I can as an encourager and helper in the exercising of her God-given talents and call.

'Years ago I had to humbly release in prayer my wife, my children, and all that I am to the perfect will of God. This has sometimes meant separation and loneliness, but it also has been the place where I am content to know that God does all things well—and rewards me with the sense of knowing that by releasing I too have done all things well and have faithfully exercised my stewardship.'

A young pastor recently said to me, 'I don't think I ever could release my wife to be away from our children and me. Her place is to take care of us.' My answer to him was, 'Even if *God* called her?'

When both a husband and wife honestly want God's will for themselves—and for each other—that divine will of God never will make them at odds. God's will never produces conflicting attitudes, beliefs, or actions. When there is conflict, there has to be human will involved—not God's.

THE SECRET OF IT ALL

The secret of harmony in a family is each of the members wanting God's will for the others instead of having their own way.

Almost fifty years of family releasing have taught me that God is not a harsh taskmaster sitting up in heaven rubbing His hands together just waiting to pounce on the one we release to Him. Oh, no! Our releasing our family members to God for His will throws open heaven's gates and allows all the blessings to flow that God has waiting up there for us. And when we decide we will allow them, they don't just trickle down. No, when we release a family member to God, then His perfect, all-knowing, for-our-good blessings will gush uninhibited from heaven—to our loved ones—and to us!

CHAPTER TEN

Prayers at Family Births

I HAD BEEN SKEPTICAL about having our almost-three-year-old granddaughter Jenna in the room for the birth of her baby sister. But her mummy and daddy, Jan and Skip, both doctors, wanted her, and had prepared Jenna month by month of the pregnancy with her own little 'baby book,' explaining such details as the 'funny stuff' that would be all over the baby, the cutting of the cord, and what that thing (clamp) was that would be sticking out of the umbilical cord. Then Jan's 'dry run' two days earlier had given Jenna and me a chance to become thoroughly acquainted with the hospital surroundings and birthing room. But I was not prepared for the deep emotional and spiritual experience that came with the birth of Crista.

Chris had come home from out of town the night before and had joined Jenna and me. The three of us stood waiting 'on the alert' outside the birthing room door during Jan's last severe contractions. Suddenly Skip opened the door and motioned us quickly in. I drew in my breath. The room was charged with imminent birth. I picked up Jenna and held her in my arms, but she recognized the steps that had

been taught her from her little book and took it all in her
stride.

But when the little head crowned, I suddenly felt the
presence of God filling the room. The shocking thing to me
was the overwhelming spiritual dimension that permeated,
yes almost saturated, the atmosphere. *Birth! God was there—
invisible, yet filling that room with His presence.* Unseen yet so
tangible. Powerful yet pleasant. Ethereal yet as real as the
air we were breathing. 'God!' my heart silently cried out
over and over.

The oneness of family was awesome. Tears trickled down
Jan's face as they laid Crista, just quickly wiped off and
wrapped in a blanket, in her arms. Jenna had asked if
people would cry, and Skip had told her, 'Yes, but they
would be tears of joy because we will be so happy—not bad
tears.'

So often in the past, and even today, birth has been
reduced to just a medical process with sterile delivery
rooms, isolation of the mother—often even from her own
husband—and whisking of the newborn off to an antisep-
tically proper nursery. How sad. How much is missed. *Birth
is God starting a new life on earth.*

Jenna had been told about the 'blood,' and it was the
only thing she didn't like about the birth. And neither did
her doctor—nor we. Suddenly, as he worked with the pla-
centa, there was a gush of blood that soaked his trousers,
shirt, shoes, the floor, and even splattered on the wall
behind him. I quickly took Jenna out into the hall, and
attendants thrust that unwashed newborn, still wrapped in
her original blanket, into Chris' arms—and they ran down
the hall wheeling Jan into the theatre. Jan had lost half of
her blood, and they were fighting to save her life.

Crista appeared shortly before noon, and we had completely ignored the time. So we decided Chris should take
Jenna to the lunchroom, and I should stay in the birthing
room with baby Crista. Everybody else was completely
engrossed in saving Jan's life.

I was totally unprepared for the next hour alone with this new baby. As I walked the floor with her, the bonding was unbelievable. I pressed her to me, talked continually, thrilled as she squeezed my finger in her little fist, and helped her suck her little finger when she cried.

But mostly I prayed. I prayed back to God the Scripture He had given me for Crista—Psalm 22:9:

> Yet Thou art He who didst bring me forth from the womb.

All through that long waiting time I had an incredible calmness and peace, praying that assurance from God over and over.

God had given me that verse on Crista's due date, August 6, 1985 after I had been praying a long time before dawn about the timing of the birth and other delivery concerns. When I had opened my Bible that morning, it was at Psalm 22; and immediately my eyes had fallen on verse 9. Instantly, I had known it was for that day—Jan's due date. And the promise to me was that it would be God's divine hands that actually would bring that baby into the world, not the hands of the obstetrician or assisting doctor/husband Skip.

But it was not until August 21 that I knew why I needed that verse from God. While they fought to save Jan's life and I walked the floor with newborn Crista, there was an incredible calmness and peace as I prayed Psalm 22:9. And it came from an unshakable faith in what God had told me fifteen days earlier *that His hands were there, and that He was in control—no matter what happened!*

Yes, God filled that room with Himself as powerfully as I ever have felt Him. But I still needed to communicate with Him—through prayer.

THE HOLY SPIRIT'S ROLE AT BIRTH

The other important prayer I prayed in that birthing room was, 'Lord, fill her with You.' I put my hand on Crista's tiny, moist hand as I prayed, 'O God, fill her with Your Spirit, Your Holy Spirit!' Then I laid my free hand on her little body as I continued to pray for her.

Through the years I have prayed many prayers about the Holy Spirit's role in my family, especially at births. Much of it I have not tried to understand theologically, but just have prayed what God spoke to me from the Bible as I read it.

All four of our granddaughters were conceived sometime before Christmas. For many years I have stayed in the Christmas story for my devotions the weeks before Christmas. Thus many of the things I prayed to God about our coming babies were from the first chapter of Luke. And I have discovered the Christmas story is so charged with the activities of the Holy Spirit.

The Christmas that Jenna and Cindy were beginning to grow as tiny foetuses, God started showing me the Holy Spirit in Luke 1. Reading about the angel promising Zacharias that the son his wife, Elizabeth, was carrying would be filled with the Holy Spirit before birth (1:15) sent me pondering my right to pray that for my grandchildren in their mothers' wombs. I realized that as the future John the Baptist, that foetus had a special calling and role on earth from God; but my heart cried out for God to give all of Himself that He intended for my grandchildren.

Also the Holy Spirit, not any human, caused the conception of Jesus in Mary. And I knew that miracle was just for Jesus, the pre-existent Son of God coming to earth. But when the second pair of cousins, Kathy and Crista, were barely on the way, I prayed, 'O God, Holy Spirit, *hover over* our little ones like You did over Mary at the Annunciation. Hover over their mothers' bodies in all You are—Your holiness, Your power, Your everything!'

And while those two cousins were being carried in their mothers' wombs at Christmastime, my prayer for them was from Isaiah 44:3: 'I will pour out My Spirit on your offspring, and My blessings on your descendants.'

And the prayer I continually pray for all of our children and grandchildren is that God will graciously pour out His Holy Spirit upon all of them.

Then it was at that same time that I prayed, 'Holy God, fill those wee new ones with the fullness of the Godhead!' based on Paul's prayer from Ephesians 3:19. And I added, 'Not for them only but, now since Pentecost, fill *all of us*— parents and grandparents—with the fullness of the Godhead so we too can be all You want us to be.'

But I also realized from Luke 1:80 that John the Baptist, although He was filled with the Holy Spirit before birth, still needed to grow and 'become strong in spirit.' I am still asking, with the crowd at John the Baptist's circumcision and naming (see Luke 1:66), 'What then will this child turn out to be?' So it is with all my grandchildren. However God chooses to answer all those prenatal prayers of mine, they still will have to grow in God—and go through the step which will give them eternal salvation—receiving Jesus as their personal Saviour and Lord. And so we still are praying that the Holy Spirit will be the implementer of God's will in their lives each day as they grow.

We now are expecting our seventh grandchild. Kurt's wife Margie is due in just three months as I write this chapter. So I have a new prayer project. And just this morning I told Margie that almost every day I pray for God to send His messenger, the Holy Spirit, to hover over, protect, and fill that little unborn one with all God wants him or her to be.

PRAYER ACKNOWLEDGES GOD'S ROLE IN MAKING BABIES

The prayers I prayed during my own pregnancies and those of all of my grandchildren were spawned from God's Words in the Bible. Some of the most meaningful and important were those cementing in my heart *Who* it was at work forming those little ones—right while it was happening.

Just days after we knew Jenna and Cindy had been

conceived, I read in Psalm 119:73: 'Thy hands made me and fashioned me.'

And my heart cried out in prayer, 'O God, it is *Your* hands making our babies.'

While my daughters and daughter-in-love have been pregnant, my almost daily prayer for the little unborn ones has been, 'O God, as each little cell multiplies, protect it from incorrect divisions and malformations which would make birth defects.' Frequently, I would pray, 'Father, today as each cell divides, make it just exactly what You want that child to be. Control the genes. Control the multiplying.'

It was when Kathy and Crista had just been conceived that I prayed back to God His assurance to me of His part in forming babies, and the horror of abortions, out of Psalm 139:13 and 16:

> For Thou didst form my inward parts;
> Thou didst weave me in my mother's womb....
> Thine eyes have seen my unformed substance;
> And in Thy book they were all written,
> The days that were ordained for me,
> When as yet there was not one of them.

SCRIPTURES FROM GOD FOR FAMILY BIRTHS

God has given me many special Scriptures for our grandchildren.

On December 3, 1984 we had a phone call from Jenna. 'We're going to have a baby,' she shouted happily into the phone. After dashing over to see the new mother and sister-to-be, Chris and I prayed together, 'Make that child all You want it to be.'

Then the next morning there was my deep prayer of thanksgiving to God. Again, Jan had had to have micro-surgery at Mayo Clinic in order to conceive this little one, and I had fretted, almost worried, that if conception didn't happen soon, the surgery would be in vain. So first I had to ask God to forgive my lack of faith. Then I prayed thanking Him, not only for the pregnancy, but that the little blob of cells in Jan's uterus was known unto Him. The potential of that life had been put there by Him, and the future planned and willed by God already.

The Scripture God gave for that future baby Crista was Psalm 78:6-7:

> That the generation to come might know, even the children yet to be born, that they may arise and tell them to their children, *that they should put their confidence in God, and not forget the works of God,* but keep His commandments (italics added).

Yes, the future baby Crista's Scripture from God!

Because Jan had paid such a high price through surgery again for her second pregnancy, newly pregnant Nancy considerately waited for a while to announce her pregnancy to us. She wanted Jan to have the limelight alone for a time. But God, without human communication, had been burdening me to pray for Dan and Nancy's baby for a couple of weeks. So I prayed strictly in obedience to God's prodding. I prayed the same prayers, asking God to fill that little one with Himself and to protect and guide and guard each division as the initial cells were budding—the same way I was praying for Jan's baby. The prayers I prayed about Psalm 139:13-16 of God forming babies in the womb before they were known were not just for Jan but also for Nancy. Then on January 10 three-year-old Cindy called to tell us they were going to have a baby. 'And it's in Mummy's inside!' she shouted over the phone. When I asked her if she loved the baby and if she was happy they were going to have a baby, I got resounding 'Yeah!' answers from her. And I got the confirmation of God's burdening me in prayer—before I even knew about the baby!

On July 14, 1985, just a month or so before Crista and Kathy would be born, the Scripture God gave for them was Psalm 100:3, 'It is He [the Lord God] who has made us, and not we ourselves.' What an assurance from God to us to know that those almost-ready-to-be-born babies were made, not only by human mothers and fathers, but actually by God!

When it was Jenna and Crista's baby brother Brett's due date, I was thrilled that God answered my prayer for his Scripture, by giving the passage immediately following Crista's in Psalm 22:9:

> Thou didst make me trust when upon my mother's breasts. Upon Thee I was cast from birth; Thou hast been my God from my mother's womb (22:9-10).

But I wept as I pondered why that coming little one would need to trust God. I then rejoiced in the promise of his, with the psalmist, *being God's from his mother's womb!* With joy and assurance I accepted from God that He would keep Brett until that time when he would be old enough to accept Jesus personally.

Grandson James' verse was special too. I had been praying for several days asking God for his verse, and on the morning of his birth September 26, 1990, God led me clearly to Psalm 121:8:

> The Lord will guard your going out and your coming in from this time forth and forever.

It was so definitely from God. And tears kept coming as deeper and deeper the words burned into my heart: 'From this time'—his birth, 'forth'—in his life, 'and forever'—to eternity. That's when God would guard him! 'O thank You, God,' I prayed, 'for so much more than I expected. I can't stop the tears from popping in my eyes and down my cheeks.'

James' mother, Margie, had been concerned about and had prayed much for her unborn child's ultimate salvation. What a thrill we both felt at God's verse for him.

RELEASING PRAYERS

Ephesians 3:20 was very special to our Margie. She had the reference engraved in Kurt's wedding ring, and even her father-in-law, Chris, had put it in his square in the quilt all the relatives had put together for a surprise wedding present for Kurt and Margie. But it became doubly significant after they had been trying to have a baby for about a year, and getting a little discouraged when she was already thirty-two. It was then Kurt and Margie prayed Ephesians 3:20 about having a baby:

> Now to Him who is able to do exceeding abundantly beyond all that we ask or think, according to the power that works within us.

'Father,' they prayed, 'this is our prayer for children—or else Your "more than we even can think or ask for." '

Margie explained, 'This was our knowing that if God didn't give us a baby, He had something even better for Kurt and me.' (It was so much like what Jan had said the night before her surgery they hoped would enable her to conceive Jenna.) 'But,' continued Margie with a grin, 'that prayer was prayed January 9, 1990, and I was already two weeks pregnant with James and didn't know it!'

There have been many difficult releasing birth prayers in my life. After my miscarried baby boy and stillborn girl, I finally released my next miscarriage when God gave me Romans 8:28—God causes all things to work together for good to those who love God, to those who are called according to His purpose.' And then there was the releasing of Judy that awful night after we had been told she could not live. But there have been others, just as difficult.

Our doctors Jan and Skip had announced her first pregnancy by knocking on our door and asking us if we wanted to see a picture of their baby. Shocked and thrilled, we said we surely did. And they promptly produced an ultrasound photo of Jan's uterus with a little blob right in the middle. 'That's our baby right there!' they beamed. But it was only two weeks later that God called on the father of that baby and me to pray a painful prayer when Jan and Skip were attending my prayer seminar in Calvary Church, St. Paul. During our learning to 'pray in God's will,' I asked everyone to think of the very most important thing to them, and then in audible prayer to give it to God for His will. I always pray what I ask the participants to pray, and immediately I knew what I had to release to God was that little blob in the ultrasound picture. With my heart breaking, I did. As soon as we finished praying, Skip dashed up to the platform and threw his arms around me. With tears in both his eyes and mine, I sobbed, 'Oh, Skip, guess what I just had to give to God!' 'I know,' he cried, 'I did too!' Releasing for God's will—the baby that He would make our Jenna!

In the spring several years later while teaching the same seminar, I came to the place of asking that we all give to God the most important thing in our lives. Immediately, I thought of the grandchildren to be born to Jan and Nancy the next summer. Flashing back into my mind were my own two spina bifida babies (one stillborn child and Judy), the cord wrapped around Cindy's neck during birth, and the possibility of physical problems with these unborn grandchildren too. But, with tears in my eyes, I prayed, 'Lord, I give to You two *normal, healthy* babies. Your will, not mine!' Two very precious possessions, released! But God gave us two bouncing baby girls—our Crista and Kathy.

Releasing prayers can, and should, end in praise because we have released that child to our God who never makes a mistake, who knows what will be best in the future, and who does all things for the good of those who love Him and are called according to His purpose. I remember finally not only releasing my second miscarriage but thanking God that He had shown us through Romans 8:28 that He was not off His throne, and this was for our good—for we could not have come back to seven more years of college and studies with three infants, Chris' father dead, and mine an invalid.

But it was not until after our stillborn and Judy had been born seriously afflicted that I began to see God's 'what ifs' in pregnancies. I was suddenly thanking Him for the termination of those two pregnancies by miscarriage—because only God knew what those babies might have been. By that time I had learned to trust God so much that thanks for His possibly avoiding a potential serious situation for Chris and me just rolled from my heart.

Psalm 100:3-5 so well expresses why we praise Him after releasing a child to Him:

> Know that the Lord Himself is God;
> It is He who has made us, and not we ourselves;
> We are His people and the sheep of His pasture.
> Enter His gates with thanksgiving,
> And His courts with praise.
> Give thanks to Him; bless His name.
> For the Lord is good;
> His loving-kindness is everlasting,
> And His faithfulness to all generations.

PRAYERS DURING BIRTH

The daughter of my secretary Sally, Sue Moore, has worked for me for several years. She just had her second baby, and I asked if she could share a very special experience she and her husband Jeff had during this baby's delivery. Sue wrote:

> When Jeff would pray aloud during my contractions, he would pray for God to relax me. God answered those prayers. I would feel the tension and fear leave me. I believe that was the major factor in cutting my labour from over sixteen hours with my first child down to less than six hours this time [although Sue delivered a nine pound, one ounce baby girl].
>
> Also as Jeff massaged my aching back, he struggled to reach down far enough on my lower back as I lay on the delivery table. 'God, somehow enable me to reach down

where it hurts!' he prayed. Soon God answered his prayer, as if giving Jeff a longer arm. I felt Jeff's hand even lower than where it hurt most! This situation made me feel that Jeff and I were not alone. It was like bringing a friend in there with us. I felt loved and cared for by *a big God!'*

Chris and I had our babies during the years fathers were basically excluded from the delivery room during the birth. But Chris' vivid memory is of his pacing the floor outside the door while I gave birth—*praying*. Although he couldn't be there to help, my husband knew well the One who could, and would, be with me—*God*.

Each of the fathers in our family could tell of their own praying for their babies. But our whole family also is involved in praying for each family birth. Developments are phoned to each other, and individually and together as families we uphold the mother, father, and new baby. We pray for God to be in control, pray for Him to ease the pain and possible fear, and at times utter prayers of deep concern. But then as the little one is born, the prayers of praise echo through the family.

A GRANDMOTHER'S PRAYERS AT BIRTH

There have been special prayers that I as the grandmother have prayed during the actual births of our grandchildren too, and the length and intensity of the prayers have been as varied as the circumstances prompting them. But always they were to include and involve the God of heaven in the very special, although sometimes a touch-and-go, event of birth.

At the due date of Nancy's first baby, Cindy, we were on vacation in Michigan. Feeling so helpless and far away, I prayed and prayed that God would let me be near her at delivery. When she started having labour pains, instead of going out fishing on Lake Michigan, I sat by a phone in town—*waiting and praying*. But those contractions, and my prayers, kept up for five days! Finally, I just flew home to be near her. (I've often wondered if that long labour was God's way of granting my prayer request.)

Nancy's Kathy was very late also. I thought I had planned the beginning of my autumn seminar schedule late enough to be sure I was there for Kathy's birth, but Nancy's being two-and-a-half weeks overdue wrecked the plans. When Kathy was born, I was on a plane en route to Omaha, Nebraska. How difficult it was for me to board that plane, and then feel it take me ever farther away from the emerging life. But being 30,000 feet in the air and hundreds of miles away did not limit me from praying. I closed my eyes so a stewardess would not bother me with drinks and food—and prayed.

Since it was just a couple of weeks after Jan's losing half of her blood at Crista's birth, I prayed for Nancy's safety. And I prayed about the lack of oxygen to the baby's brain if the cord was wrapped around this baby's neck as it was— three times—around their Cindy's. I think I prayed about everything that a grandmother who had lost four of her own babies thinks about—with anxiety and apprehension steadily growing in me. But suddenly God brought Philippians 4:6 to my mind:

> Be anxious for nothing, but in everything by prayer and supplication *with thanksgiving* let your requests be made to God (italics added).

Unsolicited and unformed by me, thanksgiving prayers welled up within me and permeated my whole being. Somehow my focus changed directions, from possible earthly problems to God. Again it was His reminding me that He is the One who takes babies from the womb.

The moment my plane landed, I dashed for the nearest phone, dialled the hospital obstetrics department, and soon I heard Kathy's healthy cry as the nurse held the phone near her! God had answered!

When Jan was due to give birth to her first child, Jenna, I asked God to teach me new dimensions in prayer. And He did. Ten days overdue, Jan had to take two eight-hour days of written internal medicine board exams, as previously mentioned in an earlier chapter. So I asked God to teach me how to pray for her through those two consecutive day's eight-hour sessions.

God started by teaching me how to persevere so long a time in prayer, first praying for my own cleansing (so I would have power in prayer) and then asking the Holy Spirit to direct my praying (so my praying would be according to God's will).

Then He taught me the reality of Jesus' hands in an amazing series of prayer events. One prayer was, 'Jesus, hold Jan's mind firmly; may there be no fear or confusion.' Also, 'Fill her mind with Your recall ability—just the amount You know she needs.' Then I asked for His hand on her writing hand, steadying, directing, legibility. Next the praying was at the piano as I sang, 'Precious Lord, take her hand; lift her up, let her stand; she is tired, she is weak, she is worn.' The next prayer was asking Jesus to put His hands of authority and power on her back, up by her shoulders. I prayed for Jesus' staying hand on the glands and chemicals that would trigger the birth process until the test was completed—for they only gave the exams once a year, and she would have to study and do it all over again the next year if not finished. As I asked God what she needed next, His answer was, 'Her lower back.' And then it was the weight on her cervix. 'O Jesus, may Your hands be like a sling under that little one, lifting its weight off Jan as she must sit all these hours.' The prayers continued with, 'She's cold. Help her, Lord,' and praying for the terrible stress on Jan's emotions and thus on the baby.

I recorded each time God told me to pray for those specific needs, and later Jan and I went over those two days. Astounded, she confirmed they were the exact times she had needed those things.

Days later Jan's labour began, and this time I asked God to teach me *how* to travail in prayer with her. And He taught me a new dimension of prayer I never had experienced before. The depth of praying was as I remembered travailing in birth, except it was spiritual. I cannot explain it, but deeply felt it while in prayer.

Brett's birth was exciting with Chris and me watching over two sisters, Jenna and Crista, in the birthing room. I hung on to both girls; but, just as Brett started emerging, I put my hands over my eyes. The nurse in charge smiled and said, 'She will be all right. She's fine.' But I knew something she did not—how Jan had lost half her blood, and almost her life, during the last delivery. But God was there again, and the joy of that new life exploded in the room. Two hours later we all celebrated with a Chinese takeaway dinner in Jan's room! Again, God was answering nine months of praying.

Prayer for Kurt and Margie's little James started when we received a 'For My Grandparents' Valentine card with an ultrasound picture enclosed. Baby Christenson apologized that it wasn't the greatest picture—but he was only six weeks old. Daily I prayed for that picture's little cluster of cells as they divided and grew. And when Margie was in labour with our little James, I prayed all the prayers I had prayed for the four preceding granddaughters. But God added one special prayer for Margie while she was in labour. I'm not sure all the kinds of labour Jesus was talking about in Matthew 11:28, but through those hours of her first labour I prayed Jesus' wonderful words for Margie:

> Come to Me, all who are weary and heavy laden, and I will give you rest.

Any woman who has given birth knows what it means to be heavy laden just before the baby comes. And the weariness of being pregnant nine months plus the fatigue experienced at giving birth are very real. But I could pray with confidence that Jesus would be there—and He would give her His rest that she so needed.

What a special time family birth is—and what a wonderful time to pray those special prayers.

BONDING PRAYERS

Bonding of caretaker adults with a newborn happens almost automatically at birth and even before birth with the mother. But bonding is important for other members of the family too. There is a special relationship that should and can develop, giving children a desperately needed sense of being loved and secure in a family relationship.

That first hour I spent with Crista while Jan was in the operating theatre produced a strong bonding. However, bonding came in a different way with Cindy and Jenna. Cindy had just been born, and Jenna was overdue when it was time for me to pack for India. I had already just wept through Jesus' words in Luke 14:33, 'So, therefore, no one of you can be My disciple who does not give up all his own possessions.' Already I had asked Him if He meant grandchildren too. And His 'yes' answer had required my difficult and tearful promise to obey Him no matter what the price—even leaving grandchildren.

Although I knew it was His will, I struggled long with leaving my first tiny grandchild, Cindy, and, even worse, perhaps my being in India when her cousin, Jenna, was born. But one of my deepest concerns was not being able to be bonded to those two little granddaughters. And adding to my uneasiness was the fact that their paternal grandmothers, Esther and Ruby, would be taking care of and getting bonded to them—instead of me.

So I prayed and prayed, asking God somehow to miraculously bond us together—while I was half way around the world from them. When I returned home from those six weeks in India, I should have been a total stranger to those two grandchildren. But I was in for a fabulous surprise. God had answered my prayers. We were, and still are, deeply bonded to each other—as grandchildren and grandmothers and grandfathers should be!

But I still had to be away from Cindy and Jenna a lot, and was concerned that we would not be as close as if I stayed near them. But God lifted that burden too. When Cindy was only three months old, at her daddy's birthday party, she wound her legs around me and threw her head back, looked me in the eye, and laughed as if to say, 'Oh, Grandma, isn't this great?' And I laughed with her, knowing it—our bonding—*was* great. *My prayers answered by God in relation to Cindy.*

Then when Jenna was eight months old, I took her in my arms after a long trip, and she too wound her legs around my waist and tucked her head into my shoulder. She just clung there—her way of saying, 'I love you, Grandma!' And I squeezed her back and whispered in her little ear, 'And Grandma loves you too, Jenna!' Bonded with Jenna!

I continually pray for bonding with all six of my grandchildren because we have to be separated by hectic schedules and distance. And I carve out every minute in my busy schedule I can to be with them, sometimes struggling because it's not as much as I would like. But the bonding is there, not from physically communicating, but from God—in answer to a grandmother's prayers.

A GIFT FROM GOD

Chris' and my praying for our family developed gradually. First we always dedicated the child of each of our seven pregnancies the moment we knew I was expecting. Then we came to the place of praying much about having babies who would be healthy and live. We also prayed for each of them throughout the pregnancy. But it was at their actual births that we especially dedicated them in prayer to God. They were His—for His will. They were His gift to us for as long as they would live. We knew well that they were the Lord's gifts to us. 'Behold, children are a gift from the Lord' (Ps. 127:3). That psalm is often quoted at birth celebrations, christenings, baby showers, and on birth announcements. And it is believed by most Christians.

But I wonder how often we actually practise what it says. Yes, children are a gift—but not from any human source. They are a gift from the Lord. So God deserves, and expects, to be included in every aspect of conception and birth.

And how do we include Him? Through prayer. Prayers of asking Him for a baby, then prayers of releasing our wills for His, prayers of protection while the baby is developing, and prayers of thanksgiving. And sometimes, when all has not gone well at the birth, there may be prayers of anger toward God, prayers telling Him of our heartache, but then eventually prayers of thanksgiving—because we know He does all things well.

CHAPTER ELEVEN

Praying When Loved Ones Die

SOMETIMES GOD DOESN'T answer our prayers about the death of a loved one the way we expect. For example, over many years I prayed asking God to let me be with my mother when she died. She had lived so close to the Lord all her life, and I wanted to see how God would usher her into His presence. Yet, always having at least 400 miles between us, I knew deep down in my heart it was unlikely I'd be near her if she died suddenly.

As we sat eating breakfast while we were vacationing in August 1986 on the shores of Lake Michigan twenty minutes drive from Mother's home, a car raced up the driveway. 'Come right away, Evelyn,' the driver shouted. 'Your mother is sick. Very sick!' Instinctively, I knew she was gone—knew I had missed her final moments on earth.

As the car seemed to crawl down the resort road toward town, questions whirled in my head. 'Why wasn't I there when I was only minutes away?' 'Why hadn't God answered my prayers by letting me be in town instead of at that cottage?' 'Why didn't that rented cottage have a phone so they could have summoned me immediately?'

I sat stunned. Had God deliberately allowed me to miss what I had prayed for all those years? Had He intentionally *not answered* my persistent prayers?

When I arrived at her house, my instincts were confirmed. Mother had died of a massive stroke. Paramedics and family had wisely decided against resuscitation. There was no way they, or I, would want to keep Mother alive mechanically. For years she had asked her prayer partners to pray that she would go fast when she died. Well, at least God had answered *their* prayers!

My sister, Maxine, and her family were standing in a silent knot in the living room, searching my eyes for answers. They motioned to the conservatory, and I walked hurriedly by them, dreading what was waiting for me. I sat down beside Mother on the couch where they had laid her and put my arms around her frail body. Holding her close, I pressed my cheek against her silver hair. And then it happened....

I felt something like electricity coming from her body. I didn't understand it, but it was there. Very real and very powerful. Almost tangible. I was acutely aware of her spirit leaving this world and entering heaven—and Mother not only hearing angels sing but singing with them. Those standing by confirmed that all I kept saying was, 'Mother, you're singing with the angels! Mother, you're singing with the angels!'

I always had thought that, no matter how strong I had been in previous disasters, I would fall apart at Mother's death. I knew deep down it would be one loss I couldn't handle. We had been too close. But there was no uncontrollable sobbing, no horrible grief, just an undeniable awareness of her entering heaven. Instead of my expected collapse, I was included in that unspeakable earth-to-heaven scene. My spiritual senses were unbelievably aware of a fantastic celestial drama.

That night as I lay in bed in the blackness, my mind raced. The angels singing. Mother singing with them. My being part of the scene. Then I began to worry. Was it all wishful thinking on my part? Did my desperate longing to be with her make me *think* I was present in the fleeting moments while life was making its final exit from her body? Was the experience really my imagination running wild?

I began to struggle with the questions again, this time praying to the Lord about them. I inquired of Him why He hadn't given us time to say our goodbyes. I questioned how He could deny a prayer request so important to me. Hadn't He understood, or even heard, all of my years of praying?

But a shock came with God's answer. Distinctly He said to my troubled soul, *'But I did answer your prayer. She waited for you!'*

Although God didn't answer it my way, He answered in a way beyond anything I ever could have imagined. God's answer was that *He let her wait for me so I could be a part of her entering heaven!*

DEATHS NOT ALL THE SAME

The next morning when I called my prayer board president to tell her Mother had died, still not understanding it, I recounted my experience at her death. 'Oh,' she replied, 'that's very much like I just read in Catherine Marshall's book about her knowing her husband, Peter, wasn't gone yet when the paramedics pronounced him dead after his fatal heart attack.' It helped some to know somebody I trusted as much as Catherine Marshall had had the same experience.

But I still wasn't satisfied. I still wondered if it all could have been just my imagination running wild—because I so wanted to be with Mother when she died. Hesitatingly, I approached our daughter Jan and recounted the story. 'Oh, that doesn't surprise me, Mother,' she responded. 'In my experience I have found that people don't all die the same. But medical science does not have the tools to measure that. As a doctor working a lot in cardiology, I have to sign many, many death certificates. But when I step into that room, it is not always the same. Sometimes there is absolutely nothing—just a body. But other times it is different. There is still something there. I can feel it. I know it.'

Then Jan added, 'Mother, that's the difference in resuscitation and just keeping a body going on pumps. Medical science can support the body's basic functions, but the person isn't alive. If you can resuscitate, bring a person back to life, then that person was not really dead. The soul had not departed.'

Jesus dealt with this at the deaths of Jairus' daughter and Lazarus. He said of Jairus' daughter, 'She has not died, but is just asleep'—and the mourners laughed at Jesus, knowing she was dead. But then Luke 8:55 says that 'her spirit returned.' Then also Jesus said to His disciples when they thought He had meant that Lazarus was just slumbering, 'Lazarus *is* dead.' And he had been dead in the tomb four days (John 11:11-14). Whatever their conditions, Jesus had power over both. And He had power to have Mother wait for me.

LISTENING PRAYERS

The most important prayers we pray during family death situations are listening prayers. Death is a time we need to *receive from God*, when we need to hear what He has to say to us.

The night my mother died, I had asked God a myriad of questions. But it was in my lying still—listening—that I received answers. It was then God, in His part of the prayer conversation, could bring His divine answers into my reeling brain, divinely settling my questions.

When we receive the news that a family member's death is inevitable (the illness is terminal), or is imminent (any moment they will go) or has occurred (too late to avoid), it is normal to bombard God with questions. Questions of Why like this? Why now? Questions of disbelief. Confused and bewildered questions. Angry questions asking God why He allowed it. Asking why He hadn't performed that miracle He was capable of doing when we had prayed for it so long. *But usually we stop at the asking, not taking time to wait on God for His answers.*

The only way we can find out how all-sufficient God can be at times like this is to *stop talking at Him* and let Him show us who He really is—the omnipotent God of heaven. Psalm 46:10 says, 'Be still, and know that I am God!' (AV)

ANSWERS FROM GOD'S WRITTEN WORD

There are times in my grief that I go directly to the Bible for the comfort and explanations I need. But many times my sorrowing brain isn't yet capable of reading. This is when God's Holy Spirit performs one of His most important tasks—recalling what Jesus has taught us previously (see John 14:25-26). This is what happened the night my mother died, and 'We do not sorrow as those with no hope' ran through my mind like an echo. It was the third member of the Trinity recalling what I had stored in my mind years before from God's Word—and needed right then.

That is one of the reasons it is so important for us to stay in God's Word—reading, studying, memorizing, hiding *His* words in our hearts. It was why when my stepfather, Rollie, died and I didn't have time to rush to my Bible for comfort on the way to the mortuary, that the Holy Spirit recalled to me, 'Why seek ye the living among the dead? He is not here, but is risen' (Luke 24:5-6, AV) as the angels spoke to the women seeking Jesus on Jesus' own resurrection morning that first Easter.

Also, if we recall Scriptures, we are sure the thoughts come from God. In times of grief our minds can play tricks on us. And we can fantasize, picturing in our imagination what we so desperately want to be true. See that loved one still alive. Or coming back to earth—perfect. That's what I found myself fleetingly doing after our little Judy died. The picture was of her decending down through the roof of the crowded church sanctuary, smiling—not paralyzed anymore—into our waiting arms. *Whole!*

But that fantasy was not from God. It was my mind helping me temporarily escape the shock. But God gently brought His truth to me, day after day and week after week, both from His continually recalling memorized Scripture to me and speaking to me directly from the Bible as I searched for His answers. It was His way of producing the real healing He knew I needed so badly. How wise for us to immerse ourselves thoroughly in His Word now, making it part of our unshakable beliefs—so that it will be ready for the Holy Spirit to use to help us when grief strikes.

PRAYERS WITHOUT WORDS

But sometimes the grief is so deep that no words will come, and there is a numbness over our whole being, making praying impossible. It is then that God comes, not with words, either, but with Himself. God did this for me after our baby girl was born dead. World War II was raging, and adequate medical treatment was scarce for civilians at home. My horrible labour had left me barely alive. An ambulance brought me to Mother's home, where I struggled with my baby's death for two days in the blackness that seemed to surround me. No words went from me to God—nor from Him to me. Just His loving filling the void with Himself. With His love, His comfort, His assurance—and His healing.

WHAT THEY SEE

When a loved one is dying, it is a time for us to see what they see. It is time for us to lift our eyes heavenward, as they so frequently do. A time for the things of this earth actually to grow dim—while the past with all its pain and heart-aches fades as the glow of heaven's gates grow brighter.

In our own family deaths, that experience has been so real. My father had been in a coma for weeks, but suddenly he rallied, looked heavenward, lifted his hands upward, as if reaching for something, and cried out, 'Jesus!' Then he fell back on his pillow—dead. Our own tiny Judy, also in a deep coma, raised the little hand that had been lifeless so long, reached toward heaven as if grasping something—and fell back—gone. I've often wondered about the angels Mother and I heard and with whom she seemed to join in singing. I did not see them. But did she—while that spark of life was fleeting from her body?

My stepfather, Rollie, spent his last day gazing intently into an upper corner of his hospital room, detached from the people and events around him. And then he went to be with the Jesus whom he had served so faithfully all his life. Our daughter Nancy told me that when she is working in the hospital with patients shortly before they die, they frequently gaze up at a corner of the ceiling. However, they are not focused on *it*—but, looking past it, their eyes are focused on *something*.

But there is a word of caution necessary here. We must not expect our loved ones to be welcomed into heaven at death if they have not received Jesus as their Saviour and Lord. When Jesus in John 14 told His disciples He was going to prepare a place for them (who believed in Him), Thomas said, 'Lord, we do not know where You are going, how do we know the way?' Then Jesus so clearly but definitely answered with:

> *I am the way,* and the truth and the life; *no one comes to the Father but through Me* (John 14:6, italics added).

What do believers see? Is it the place Jesus said He was going to prepare for His followers? The many dwelling places, mansions, Jesus told them were in His Father's house? They certainly see more than the tunnel so many unbelievers see at death. More than even the bright light at the end of that tunnel. No, if they really have their names written in the Lamb's Book of Life (see Rev. 21:27) by truly receiving Jesus as their Saviour, they are seeing the glories of their new home in heaven.

Our family had gathered for a private visitation at the mortuary that summer Sunday morning before my mother's afternoon funeral. The windows of a neighbouring church were open, and suddenly their trumpet ensemble triumphantly filled the air with the song 'We Shall Behold Him.' Our Nancy told me that she had the overwhelming feeling of the heavens opening up and the song being fulfilled—as she *knew* Grandma was beholding her Saviour.

GOD'S VIEW OF DEATH

When I left Minnesota for India in 1990, all our family members were healthy. Death was far from my thinking. But a phone call that finally got through to me in Calcutta changed all that. My husband's mother was in a coma— and none of the doctors expected her to live. I had to leave immediately for Hyderabad, struggling whether to go on with the just-started national tour or fly home immediately. My seminar coordinator, Juliet Thomas, slipped me a little note just before the seminar which I hadn't had time to read. In the wings of that auditorium in Hyderabad, I was trying to collect my composure as my heart was reeling over the news I had just received. Facing all day of teaching that large crowd, I sat on a stool staring at the floor, trying to switch my thinking from Grandma Chris to what I was to teach. Remembering Juliet's note, I opened it and read, 'Psalm 116. Evelyn, this psalm is so precious to me.' As I hurriedly turned to the psalm in my Bible and began reading, my eyes immediately fell on verse 15:

> Precious in the sight of the Lord is the death of His godly ones.

Suddenly my heart focused not on Minnesota, nor India, but on heaven. And on God—sitting up there with a smile on His face, so happy that one of His choice servants was close to coming to Him. And all my feelings turned upside down. I saw God's view of death, not the human side of losing a loved one we all were feeling. God's side of joyously and anxiously awaiting His beloved's homecoming.

THANKFUL PRAYERS AT DEATH

As the death of a family member comes closer, often there is pleading in prayer with God to let the loved one stay just one more day, or week, or month. And often drastic medical procedures are put in operation to fulfil this desire. And then, when that dear one has departed, many kinds of grieving prayers follow. God expects us to grieve, and knows our emotional well-being depends on it. But sooner or later in these steps there should come one more step in the death praying—*thankfulness!* Thankfulness? For what?

My telephone prayer chain chairman, Jeanne, had been taking care of her dying ninety-five-year-old mother. But when she died and the funeral was over, Jeanne said to me, 'I miss her so terribly. But, amazingly, I have a tremendous sense of *thankfulness* engulfing me. Thankfulness for her just slipping into another phase of her life. Mother has not died but is just in a continuation of her life in another place. Oh, I'm so thankful.'

Going back to visit my mother's home two years after her death, I was surprised at a spirit of thankfulness that kept sweeping over me—still missing her so much, but engulfed by an attitude of thankfulness. Why? Revelation 21:4 once again was real to me:

> And He shall wipe away every tear from their eyes; and there shall no longer be any death; there shall no longer be any mourning, or crying, or pain.

I think of three loved ones especially in that connection. My mother, as I have mentioned, had a very hard life. My dad was an invalid for years. Our little Judy's partially paralyzed body gradually could not handle the escalating fever that turned her from red to the final deep purple. And many, many times I have prayed thanking God that they now are experiencing life without the hassles and pain of that reassuring Bible verse.

When my loved ones have died, I have uttered prayers of

thankfulness to Jesus because He, by His death and resurrection, put an end to the agony of death (Acts 2:24). I have thanked Him that through death He rendered powerless the devil who had the power of death (Heb. 2:14). And I have breathed prayers of thankfulness because Jesus delivered those who through fear of death were subject to slavery all their lives (Heb. 2:15). 'Thank You, Jesus!'

> O death, where is thy sting? O grave, where is thy victory? (1 Cor. 15:55, AV)

Another surprising thankfulness came when my mother was just in the middle of reading my then just-released book *What Happens When God Answers*—and suddenly died. Immediately, I was so sorry that she had not finished the book because I had so wanted her to read in the final pages about where all of her lifelong prayers were preserved and enhanced in golden bowls in heaven. Then I stopped short. 'O Lord,' I prayed, 'thank You that she doesn't have to read it in a book. *Thank You that now she sees those prayers of hers You have preserved until the final day.* (See Rev. 5:8 and 8:3-4.)

Also, when a loved one who faithfully has supported us in prayer dies, we feel a terrible loss. How can we thank God in prayer for that? Mother was our family's powerful prayer supporter, and that loss flooded over me—until I focused on how God actually handles answering prayers. He never stamps 'case closed' after He initially answers, but He continues answering and answering as long as is needed. Although there is nothing in the Bible about Mother praying new prayers now, I was able to pray, *thanking God that I would still be the recipient of all those years of Mother's prayers for me.*

One day in her latter years I lovingly told her, 'Mother, you can't die!' Startled, she asked why not. 'Because I need you to pray that prayer you pray for me every day—that I won't get proud.' But God is still using that prayer in my life to this day.

When Nancy, still in her deep grief, wondered if

Grandma, now that she was up in heaven, could see her, I
answered, 'I don't know that, Nancy; but I do know that all
of those prayers she prayed for you will follow you throughout your life.'

Reunion in heaven is another reason for my prayers of
thankfulness. Is my mother holding Judy in her arms now?
Oh, how she loved Judy! And holding our stillborn baby
girl? Mother was the one who stayed with me the two full
days of terrible labour—and then picked out Judy's pret-
tiest dress to bury her in. And then that first miscarriage
when Mother so carefully put that little boy foetus in a blue
velvet jewelry box and buried him in the shade of the tree in
our garden. Are they all together in heaven—singing and
shouting together? I believe they are. 'O Father, *thank You!*'

WHAT MY MOTHER LEFT BEHIND
One of my deepest prayers of thanks at Mother's death was
for what she left behind. When we went through her possessions, everything we found was about one of two things—
Jesus or her family. All of her books, magazines, songbooks,
letters, notes, pictures, and even her chequebook were
exclusively either for family or her Lord.

Her personal belongings reflected the Apostle Peter's
words about what he had taught them when he knew 'the
laying aside of [his] earthly dwelling' (death) was imminent: 'And I will also be diligent that at any time after my
departure you may be able to call these things to mind' (2
Peter 1:14-15). Mother truly left us the heritage Steve Green
sings about in Jon Mohr's song 'Find Us Faithful.'

> After all our hopes and dreams have come and gone,
>   And our children sift through all we've left behind;
> May the clues that they discover,
>   And the memories they uncover,

> Become the light that leads them
>> To the road we each must find.*

Discovering at Mother's death all these godly personal things made my heart swell with thankfulness to God for her. And it multiplied my resolve to be and do the same for my children and all who come behind me.

In much the way I remember my mother, my husband, Chris, has special memories of his father, Rudolph, an unusually godly man and a man of prayer. When Chris was almost three years of age, the Christenson family moved into a brand new home, and one day before the large lawn and paths were laid, Rudolph came in for lunch. Behind him came little Chris, struggling to put each foot where his father had made tracks. Triumphantly, he announced, 'Look, Mummy, I came all the way home in Daddy's footprints!' And my prayer still is, 'O thank You, God, for giving Chris and me such godly examples. May we always be the people of deep devotion and prayer as were my mother and Chris' father and mother.'

VICTORY PRAYERS AT DEATH

Several hours later in that sleepless night after Mother died, I prayed a lot more 'death prayers.' Prayers that many Christians have prayed when a loved one has gone to heaven.

Experiencing a strange peace and lack of wrenching grief, I prayed, 'Lord, I'm supposed to be devastated. But the terrible void is filled with something so positive.' Then apprehension filled my heart as I remembered that one of the steps of grief is not facing reality. 'O God,' I cried out in

---

the darkness, 'am I not facing reality? Is my mind playing tricks on me?' But God lifted my fears by gently, yet very clearly, bringing to my mind Scripture I had used so many times as a pastor's wife to comfort a loved one left behind. The Scripture that also was to be mine when I had been left without her. From God Himself was the explanation for my lack of devastating grief:

> But we do not want you to be uninformed, brethren, about those who are asleep [have died], that you may not grieve, as do the rest who have no hope (1 Thes. 4:13).

Why no deep grieving? Because we have hope—hope in Jesus that those without Him do not have. And we not only have the hope of being together again with them for eternity, but the awesome scene that Paul described next to use to comfort each other—when Jesus comes back:

> For if we believe that Jesus died and rose again, even so God will bring with Him those who have fallen asleep in Jesus....For the Lord Himself will descend from heaven with a shout, with the voice of the archangel, and with the trumpet of God; and the dead in Christ shall rise first. Then we who are alive and remain shall be caught up together with them in the clouds to meet the Lord in the air, and thus we shall always be with the Lord (1 Thes. 4:14, 16-17).

AN EXPERIENCE MARGIE RECALLS

Kurt's wife, Margie, at first hesitated sharing the extraordinary experience she and her family had at her brother Bob's death (see chap. 9) because, she said, 'It seems like such a special gift given personally to my family who needed extra encouragement from a very loving Heavenly Father.' But she decided to recount the experience because 'it illustrates how much hope and joy there can be in mourning. They can coexist,' she pointed out, 'but mourning must rest on the foundation of the hope that we have in

Jesus—or despair will become too great.' She recounts the experience as follows:

> Even in death, the hand of God can reach out to the true believer in comfort and compassion hard to comprehend. The night my brother Bob died, none of us wanted to go to bed and be alone. So we pushed two double beds together. But before my parents and we three sisters lay our heads down, we knelt and prayed as we had done so often during my brother's illness. We prayed for peace and the ability to sleep. And peace came—almost like a thick, heavy blanket lying across the room. God's peace—safe, warm, secure, the kind that 'surpasses all comprehension' (Phil. 4:7).
>
> But God had more for us. The night of my brother Bob's funeral, two high school friends of my older sister were walking in the park. Rich was a good friend of the family, but Kevin only knew of our struggle with Bob's illness; he never had seen Bob. As they walked and talked of the day's events, Rich suddenly stopped, seemingly frozen and unable to move. They both felt a strange presence. Kevin grabbed Rich's arm and explained a vision he was seeing. Two people, he said, were in the clear, late summer sky, both bright and shining. One seemed to be Jesus and the other was a boy with blond, shining hair. His young face was bright and full of light; it was hard to see detailed features, but the shape and hair were distinct.
>
> Rich and Kevin ran to our house and Dad opened the door. I saw them standing there still quite wide-eyed and shaken, telling us what they had seen. Dad grabbed Bob's graduation picture, and Kevin said yes, that was the boy with Jesus in the night sky!
>
> We were filled with awe and wonder at the vision. Why was God so kind as to send the vision to a hurting, grieving family? I don't know why, but we know that God did—and He is sovereign. I'm also sure, although we already knew it from Scripture, that God wanted us to be assured that in death the righteous have a refuge (see Prov. 14:32). He wanted us to know we don't travel through death's door alone as if it were an uncharted journey. *No, Jesus is there!*

CORONATION, NOT CULMINATION

Death has periodically stalked our family. Two miscarriages and a stillbirth in between, the later occurring just five weeks after my husband's father's death. A few years later while attending a convention in Amsterdam, Holland, I felt an overwhelming urge to call home. My cheery 'hello' turned to chilling silence as Mother related the horrifying details of my nephew's murder. He was the only son of my only brother. Mother rehearsed for me how a large object had been deliberately dropped on him while he was inspecting a construction site after hours. My thoughts had raced across the Atlantic to his pregnant wife, Stephanie. What was the shock doing to her? To the unborn baby? Two weeks later the baby was born to Stephanie, and they called to tell Mother of the birth. But it was the last phone call my mother received. Minutes later she was dead.

But through it all there was victory. As my husband preached Mother's funeral service, he had us all pick up the obituary we had been handed as we came in, and said, 'You are not holding in your hand an obituary. You are holding a *ticket to a coronation*. This is not the culmination of Edna Moss' life, but rather a coronation—a victory celebration as one of God's choice servants enters His presence. Our victory prayer: Coronation—not culmination!

> And the righteous will shine forth as the sun in the kingdom of their Father (Matt. 13:43).

CHAPTER TWELVE

Special Prayers for Special Times

GREETING CARD STORES bulge with cards of best wishes, good cheer, good luck, and blessings for every conceivable occasion and for every taste. People spend large amounts of time and money reaching other people on their special days. Being remembered at special times of our lives is extremely important. It can cheer us up, make us grateful for friends, appreciative of their thoughtfulness, and even raise our self-esteem because we were important to someone. All of this is good. But the source of all of these wishes is human, and has little or no power actually to produce what was wished for them in the greeting.

But there is a communication on special days that is beyond the human sphere. It really can bring to the recipient what was desired by the sender. It is called prayer.

Prayer for special people on their special days brings God's input into their lives. Our 'best wishes' actually turn into divine influence, divine favour, and divine blessings— *when we pray.*

FAMILY MEMBERS' SPECIAL DAYS

Through the years I have prayed special prayers for each family member on his or her special days. It is that individual's 'intercessory prayer day.' I set aside a special time for each family member when it is his or her birthday, wedding day, graduation day, or any other important day that comes along. That loved one gets the bulk of my intercessory prayertime that day.

However, these are not just my human wishes for them. No. Before I start praying for them, I stay in prayer asking God to direct me to a special Scripture *He has for them for that special occasion.* Sometimes this takes several days. And, when God either calls a Scripture to my mind for the person or stops me in my devotional reading on a verse for the individual, that is what I pray for that family member. Special day prayers are very precious to me.

FAMILY BIRTHDAY PRAYERS

God has given me inumerable birthday prayers for my husband, children, grandchildren, mother, father, sister, and brother. Some birthday prayers God has given me have been quite special.

It was the summer of 1988, and Jenna was the first granddaughter for whom God gave me a very special birthday verse. All my granddaughters were having birthdays within a few weeks, and I had been praying for their birthday verses for quite a while. Jenna's came on July 18, two months before I would need it to include in my intercessory prayer for her—and give to her on her birthday card.

The summer before Cindy and Jenna each had given me a feather very important to them. Jenna's was a multicoloured peacock feather which I had randomly tucked in my Bible at the thirty-first chapter of Proverbs. Many times I had seen that feather as I turned to something else in my Bible, and always had stopped to pray at least a short prayer for Jenna, frequently stroking the silky feather while I prayed.

But on that early summer day as I sat praying on the empty Lake Michigan beach, I felt compelled to pray for Jenna's birthday verse. So I turned to Proverbs 31 and Jenna's feather, and immediately my eyes fell on the last half of verse 30:

> A woman who fears [reverences] the Lord, she shall be praised.

I tried to read and apply the first part of that verse, 'Charm is deceitful and beauty is vain,' but somehow it didn't fit. It was not what God was giving me for Jenna. Later her mother, Jan, became almost alarmed thinking that God might have been saying that negative side too. But I assured her that, no matter how hard I tried to read the whole verse, God definitely said it was the last half about the woman who reverences the Lord being praised.

What a wonderful verse for a precious little girl just beginning to grow into womanhood. What a promise for the future from God—that if she would reverence Him, she would be praised. Not praised for her charm or beauty, which are only deceitful and vain, but praised for her beautiful life of reverencing the Lord! *My birthday prayer for Jenna!*

Cindy's special feather came the summer of 1987 too. We were walking on the Lake Michigan beach, and she became fascinated by the seagull feathers and started a collection of them. She gave me one of her prize feathers which I put in my Bible, and every time the next year I saw that feather as I opened my Bible, I would pray for Cindy. While away from her in the middle of the next winter, I found myself gently running my fingers over that soft feather, remembering doing the same over her soft little face as I had prayed for her that summer.

Amazingly, the place I had tucked Cindy's feather that previous summer was also where God had her 1988 birthday verse waiting. Again as I walked that same beach, the seagull feathers strewn in my path were a reminder to pray for Cindy, which I did. When I sat down to read the Bible, I instinctively turned to Cindy's feather. And there it was, positively, from the Lord. Almost jumping off the page at me. Cindy's next birthday promise:

For you will go out with *joy* (Isa. 55:12).

But little did I understand how important God knew that verse would be to Cindy. It was not until several months later that an upset Cindy called and announced firmly, 'Grandma, I have a new name. My name is "Rebecca" now. I wanted a Bible name, but my parents didn't name me a Bible name. And I don't like my name "Cynthia Joy" because it isn't in the Bible. So I just changed it.'

'Oh, darling,' I replied, thrilled at her wanting a Bible name but also sensing the urgency of the situation, 'don't you remember your feather and birthday verse from Isaiah 55:12, "For you will go out with *joy*"? You do have a Bible name. "Joy" is mentioned more times in the Bible than any name given to anybody. Look at that picture on your wall spelling J-O-Y from the Bible that Grandma gave you. And remember how the angel said to the shepherds that first Christmas that he was bringing good news of great "joy" for all people—the Baby Jesus. And, honey, the second fruit of God's Holy Spirit in us is "joy". The Bible is full of the word *joy*.'

Year after year I pray for that joy for Cindy. And just last summer (1991) God gave me another dimension of her birthday joy for now nine-year-old Cindy. Whose joy would be hers? Jesus' joy that He left for us on earth! And, amazingly, it was His joy when He was ready to go to the cross (John 15:11). When I told Cindy about the new dimension of her birthday verse and explained that it was Jesus' joy during a sad time when He was ready to go to the cross, Cindy thoughtfully replied, 'Grandma, Jesus gave them His joy because He wouldn't need it anymore in heaven!'

No, Jesus wouldn't need that kind of joy in a perfect heaven, but He knew Cindy would down here on earth.

Many, many times I have prayed that prayer for Cindy, and many times, too, when things were difficult, I've reminded her of her precious name and birthday gift from Jesus—*joy*.

TWO MORE BIRTHDAY PRAYERS

Crista and Kathy were just turning three that summer of 1988 when God gave me those special birthday verses for Jenna and Cindy. And He had one for Crista and Kathy too.

Crista's verse puzzled me at first because it seemed so mature and advanced for such a little girl. But I knew it was from God, and I wrote on her birthday card: 'Dear Crista: I prayed and asked God for a birthday Bible verse for you. Then I turned to the page where I was ready to read my Bible that day, and immediately my eyes fell on these words for you:

> Blessed are those who hear the Word of God, and observe it (Luke 11:28).

'Crista, that means that God wants you to listen to His words in the Bible, and then do what they say. Darling, that will make you a strong Christian and make God very happy. I love you, darling, with all my heart. Grandma.'

The 'on the contrary' that starts Crista's verse shows Jesus is answering the woman who, in the preceding verse, had said, 'Blessed is the womb that bore You, and the breasts at which You nursed.' But Jesus said, 'No, it is those who hear the Word of God and obey it who are blessed.'

As Crista has grown older, the 'why' of this verse is becoming more clear. Not only is it quite difficult for a child to screen out all the sources of wisdom vying for their little minds (see James 3:15), but really obeying God's Word isn't taught much any more, even in many Christian circles. Somehow we have taken 2 Timothy 3:16 to read, 'All Scripture is inspired by God and is profitable for teaching' and have stopped there. We have forgotten that it says that teaching ('doctrine,' AV) must be applied because Scripture also is good 'for reproof,' 'for correction,' and 'for training in righteousness.' For Crista, God was saying that as she grows up He wants her to listen to His words in the Bible, for correct doctrine to be sure, but then also to obey what it said. Then she will be blessed in His sight. What a tall order for a little girl. But what a precious privilege to have God tell her what will make her blessed! *What a birthday prayer for Crista.*

On Kathy's birthday in 1988 I was very concerned that God had given me a Scripture verse for all the other grand-daughters, but nothing definite for her. On her birthday in her special prayertime, for some reason I had kept praying claiming the blood of Jesus against Satan harming her. Then I prayed and prayed for God to send His angels to protect her. Then I prayed for His angels to surround her. The day after her birthday it was still the same kind of praying, even asking God to give it only when it was His time. God even had rebuked me out of Luke 12:26 about being anxious as I kept asking about it. However, the third day after her birthday while praying for her, I suddenly realized that *God had given me Kathy's birthday Scripture.* I had been praying it all those three days!

> He will give His angels charge concerning you, to guard you in all your ways (Ps. 91:11).

Kathy's birthday verse actually was two verses. God first brought to my mind Hebrews 1:14, 'Are they [the angels] not all ministering spirits, sent out to render service for the sake of those who will inherit salvation?' But that was only to remind me of the explanation of God's task for angels. Psalm 91:11 was Kathy's special verse.

Kathy's birthday verse came vividly into focus for that little girl, and us, two years after God gave it in 1988. After a meeting in Washington, D.C., I had stayed two extra days to be with their family for Monday the Fourth of July. On the way home from church, I sat between the girls in the back seat of the car, and we read in the Bible and discussed their individual birthday verses—joy and angels. Kathy had asked, 'What do angels do, Grandma?' And we talked how they protect us from harm.

The next morning Dan, Nancy, the girls, and I drove through the Blue Ridge Mountains to Luray Caverns for our holiday outing. Driving up a narrow mountain road with almost no shoulders, we rounded a blind curve. To our horror a truck straddling the central line appeared right in front of our car. Suddenly the truck swerved several feet in our direction—facing us head on. Dan furiously jerked the steering wheel, violently tossing us all about—and the truck narrowly missed us. After getting settled and catching our breath, we talked about and thanked God for the angels protecting us *right then*.

After seeing the cavern, we drove out into the mountain country to eat dinner in a 200-year-old farm house, now a restaurant. After playing with their beautiful horses and kittens, we got in the car to go home. Pulling out onto that mountain back road, Dan and Nancy had both looked carefully both ways, and there were no cars. But just as we got across the road while turning left up the hill, a car shot over and down that hill travelling at least sixty miles an hour. As the driver slammed on the brakes, the car fish-tailed several times, barely missing us twice. As Dan jammed our car into reverse, the other car came to a stop right in front of ours. When the shock subsided a little, we remembered the angels. This time their reality and thanks for them were much more vivid in our minds. It had become obvious to all of us that we really did need—and had had—*God's angels protecting us*.

God has given me many more Scriptures about the angels protecting us through these years; and, because God knew we would need them, I have prayed them for all of us.

BIRTHDAY PRAYERS FOR BOYS

James and Brett were yet unborn when God gave me those special birthday verses for our four granddaughters. But it was at the births of these grandsons that God so clearly showed me their verses.

On Brett's due date, I was reading devotionally in Psalm 51, and read, 'The sacrifices of God are a broken spirit; a broken and a contrite heart, O God, Thou wilt not despise' (v. 17). Remembering Jan's near-death experience while giving birth to her last child, Crista, I wept over this Scripture. But then I prayed, 'O God, if this is not the Scripture for this new baby, please give it to me.'

And it wasn't! He firmly guided me to Psalm 22; and, surprisingly, to the words immediately following the assurance of 'Yet Thou art He who didst bring me forth from the womb' (v. 9a) that had taken me through that first hour after Crista's birth while they were fighting to save our Jan's life. I wept again, only a different kind of tears, as God clearly gave me the words (vv. 9b-10) for our soon-to-be baby Brett Jezreel Johnson.

> Thou didst make me trust when upon my mother's breasts. Upon Thee was I cast from birth; Thou hast been my God from my mother's womb.

My apprehension as to why that baby would have to trust while an infant, and why it would be cast upon God at birth, soon turned to the wonderful promise that God would be its God from its mother's womb! And the day Brett was born, I prayed with joy and victory in my heart—knowing that God was his God.

James' verse came from God also after I prayed several days over and over for God to give it to me. On September 26, 1990, God finally said 'Psalms,' and I turned to Psalm 121 where He seemed to be leading. I recorded in my Bible, 'Strong tears. Very definite at verse 8.'

The Lord will guard your going out and your coming in from this time forth and forever.

The tears just kept coming and coming as these words went deeper and deeper into my heart. My question of 'When will the Lord guard his going out and coming in?' was answered: 'From this time'—at his birth, 'forth'—on into his life, and 'forever'—to eternity. I wrote it in capital letters with three exclamation points. God's assurance in my heart for James' eternity! The promise engulfed my whole body as I wept before God. 'Oh, thank You, Lord,' I prayed with overwhelming and surprised thankfulness. This verse was so much more than had been expected, I couldn't stop the tears from flowing down my cheeks.

As I write, baby boy/girl Christenson is due soon. Kurt and Margie's second baby, our seventh grandchild, is on the way. And I can't wait to see what Scripture God has for that little one at birth!

BIRTHDAY CELEBRATIONS

Birthdays always have been very special at our house. Every birthday person gets breakfast in bed, and is king or queen for that day. We decorate the house with balloons and streamers, and brightly decorate the pile of gifts. We either use the best china and silver or a carefully selected theme of birthday plates, napkins, and tablecloth. Then we let the birthday person choose his or her favourite foods and birthday dessert, and gather together as many members of the family who possibly can be there to celebrate. I can recall many times of feeling overwhelmed at the expressions of love and being loved—in the warmth of the glow of those birthday candles.

But amidst all that, there is something much more important that we do. We always include the *birthday prayer*. This is giving thanks to God for giving us that special person, and then evoking God's special blessing on him or her for the coming year. This usually is prayed by an 'elder' of the family—father, mother, grandfather, grandmother, or great grandmother.

Grandma Chris is the one we call on to pray for her children. Now that she's ninety-two, she has prayed these blessings on her own children up to a seventieth birthday for her son, Chris. An especially meaningful one was when he turned sixty-five, and Grandma Chris thanked God for His bountiful mercy and guidance through all those years, and then evoked God's blessing and direction for Chris in his retirement years.

One of the most meaningful birthday prayers of our family was prayed in July 1986 by my mother, Grandma Moss. All of her great grandchildren had gathered at a cottage on Lake Michigan for a rare combined big birthday party. Those great grandchildren were very precious to Grandma Moss, and she had lived sacrificially for them and her grandchildren and her children all of her life. So we were thrilled to have her there at age ninety-one to pray for that collection of her great grandchildren, captured for us all on video tape.

Holding baby Crista on one hip, she surveyed her rich family possessions, and raised her voice to the God she knew so well. 'As we look to Thee at this time, God, we have so many things to thank You for.' Then, flowing from the depths of her being came, 'We begin, Lord, by thanking Thee that Thou hast privileged us to be together today. So many of our family are here....' Next came her deep lifelong goal for herself and goal for all her family line. 'And we want to make Thee first in our lives, and we want to please Thee in everything we do and everything we say.'

And, before thanking God for the wonderful food and all the hands that had prepared it, Grandma Moss prayed the last thing she ever prayed in public for anyone. *Her blessing for her offspring.*

'And, God, we just ask Thee to bless each one and bless these, especially these that are having their birthdays. God, we ask Thee to come and bless their lives, and help them to grow up to be wonderful Christian men and women. And we'll give Thee the praise and the glory. Amen.' At the end of that week Grandma Moss died of a massive stroke. That birthday prayer was her final blessing!

JESUS' BIRTHDAY

The first celebration a child seems to become aware of is his or her own birthday with blowing out of candles and family members singing 'Happy Birthday.' Sensing our first child Jan's grasping of the specialness of birthdays, we decided to help her understand Christmas by having a birthday cake with candles for Jesus.

Through the years that has been a part of our family Christmas celebration—the birthday cake or fancy dessert for Jesus, candles to blow out for Jesus, the singing of 'Happy Birthday Dear Jesus' and the *birthday prayer* we prayed about Jesus just as we prayed for them on their birthday. At first the prayer was just thanking Jesus for being born on earth, then it progressively got deeper as the children matured spiritually—until they could understand thanking Him for being our Saviour and for saving us from our sins.

This celebration taught our little ones so much. Early in life it made them aware of Jesus being a real person, and that Jesus' birthday was just as important to Him as ours was to us. They learned to give Jesus the love we received on our birthdays. It cemented in their little minds that Christmas was about Jesus' birth and not Santa Claus or presents. And it made Jesus that extra special Person, King for a day—and then eventually King of every day of their lives.

MAKING CHRISTMAS SPECIAL—FROM JAN

All of our family homes have special day observances that have become a tradition. And Chris, as a pastor much of his adult life, kept our whole family deeply aware of the spiritual significance of each holiday through his preaching and emphasis in the church's entire calendar. But since fifty years of marriage have produced far too many celebration prayers to put in one book, I have touched on only a few.

Our daughter Jan comments as follows:

Special days are wonderful. Holidays cause us to focus on concepts that are lost in the turmoil of day to day family life. When our children were very small, Father Christmas was a major figure in their lives. But I felt a deep desire to explore with them the fundamentals of our faith through the Christian truths of holidays.

It amazes me the depth with which children think and their ability to understand profound spiritual concepts. So much time and energy is rightly spent on intellectual stimulation for our children. But they need adequate spiritual stimulation so as not to stunt their God-ordained growth, and develope into spiritually underprivileged kids.

However, children often understand ideas better when they are graphically displayed. Jesus knew this and so He spoke in parables to all of us. Special days give us a chance to translate concepts into 'visual parables' so that, before we try to pray in abstract terms with our children, they already will understand the concepts of our special-day praying.

Christmas is one of those wonderful, special times—a time of family gatherings. I'm struck, however, by how much we lose when we leave Jesus in the manger. Christmas is not about a baby. It is the beginning of the unfolding of God's plan for redemption, the opening scene of His Passion Play. To focus only on the Babe in the manger and the surrounding events, as miraculous as they are, is to lose sight of *who* that Baby was. He was not a sweet little baby boy; He was the omnipotent, victorious Saviour of the universe. Only when we understand this can we begin to comprehend the truly incredible nature of what happened in Bethlehem.

Weeks before Christmas, rather than using the usual advent calendar and candles, our family begins our journey through the four times we feel Christ comes to the believer—His 'advents' if you will—and we light each week's candle at our special Sunday morning breakfast.

The first morning of our 'advents' we light the pink

candle as one child says, 'Jesus came in the flesh.' Then we pray thanking the Son of God for His coming in the flesh and giving up heaven to take on the pain of humanity for us.

The second time Christ comes is to a person in salvation when he or she actually receives Him as Saviour. After lighting the red candle on those mornings, another child says, 'Jesus comes to us with His blood.' Then we pray thanking Him for His saving blood. We have had many good discussions among all of us about what that means to us personally and what Jesus did to make that possible.

Christ also comes for the believer he or she dies—our third week's topic. Jenna chose a light blue candle for us to light this day. A child then says, 'Jesus comes for us when we die.' The concept of death has fascinated our children, and this has given us opportunities to talk about what death is—and what it isn't. We then pray together thanking God for His provision for eternal life with Him.

The last time Christ comes to the believer is when He returns to earth in final judgment. As we light this white candle, a child repeats, 'Jesus comes for us at the final judgment.' What a great picture we can, and do, paint of a victorious Christ coming in all His glory for us, and Satan forever defeated. *Now we are ready for Christmas.*

On Christmas Eve our whole extended family gets together, and after dinner we read in unison the Christmas story from Luke 2. Then we discuss what Jesus would like for a birthday present. The children decide (sometimes with help) that He wants our hearts. But our hearts are dirty, and we can't give someone a dirty birthday present. So, under each plate is a red heart with a black sticker on it. We have a quiet time when people ask God for forgiveness for the 'black spot.' Then they peel it off, throw it into the blazing fireplace, and then put their clean heart in a box wrapped like a birthday present. When everyone is finished, the children put the box under the Christmas tree and sing 'Happy Birthday, Dear Jesus.' It's a sweet, introspective time that I treasure and the girls love to set up.

MY FIRST GRANDMOTHERING CHRISTMAS
The first Christmas Eve we had grandchildren, the joy and love flowing was incredible. The thrill of soft cuddly toys

and clothes, and the babies having more fun with the pretty wrappings than with their gifts, made that Christmas truly special. But when the festivities died down, I had the wonderful privilege as a new grandmother of putting each of our new babies to bed. But on such a special night as that, I didn't waste it on Santa and reindeer stories or even on singing Christmas carols as lullabies. No, this was the time for *special Christmas prayers*.

As Jenna snuggled, burrowing herself into my arms, I laid my hand on her and prayed out loud. First it was 'Happy Birthday, Jesus.' Then I thanked God for Jenna, asked Him again to fill her with His Holy Spirit, and kissed her long on that forehead I loved so much.

How precious it was to rock baby Cindy to sleep that night while she snuggled. I held her close and thanked her for all the hugs and pats she had given me that evening. And then I laid my hand on her too and prayed that God would fill her and make her exactly the girl He has planned for her to be. Again it was that special time of prayer for that special night in her life. Christmas praying!

EASTER AT SKIP AND JAN'S HOUSE
Jan tells of Easter in the Johnson home:

> Of all the holidays Easter is the pivotal point of our faith. Somehow, though, it can get lost in bunnies, eggs, and new dresses. Not to say that those things are all bad—we have bunnies and eggs, and sometimes new dresses. But I felt the emphasis needed to be refocused on the real issues of Easter.
>
> Easter without the risen Christ exploding out of the tomb is an impotent holiday. Our preparation for this special day begins several weeks before Easter when Skip brings the hand-hewn six-foot cross into our large front hall and we hang our purple 'veil' on the wall near it. That hall connects all the areas of our house, and sometimes when I catch just a glimpse of one of these Easter reminders, it brings a whole flood of thoughts about the price our Lord paid for my sin. And I offer up a prayer of grateful adoration through my tears.

Our dining table holds our crown of thorns with four candles signifying the concepts of redemption. Every year as I work the candles into this centrepiece, I invariably prick my fingers. And, as I wipe off the blood, my mind drifts back to Jesus' bleeding body.

The Sunday we light the first candle, we thank God for His plan for redemption. How awesome it is to realize that I am important enough to Him to die for. And He never gives up on us. On Palm Sunday we light a purple candle reminding us of Jesus' triumphal entry, and together hail the King of Kings, Jesus.

Good Friday is always a powerful time for us as we light the blood red candle and ask God for the outpouring of Jesus' blood on our family. There is power in the blood, and it hangs heavy in the air as we proceed. Standing before the cross with four-inch spikes and hammer, we nail red ribbons symbolizing our sins to the cross. It seems almost unbearable as we listen to the blows of the hammer. What must it have been like the first time! I have no response but to kneel at the foot of the cross and plead for the blood to keep covering my sins.

Then we have Communion as a family seated on the floor between the cross and the purple veil. What tender times we have had discussing forgiveness and the meaning of the veil being rent in two like the veil of the temple was supernaturally torn from top to bottom when Christ died. It was at this time that three-year-old Crista prayed, 'I'm sorry, God, for breaking Your rules.' Together we pray, thanking God for His almost unbelievable act of love. Then we rip our veil in two from top to bottom.

Easter morning dawns, and our white candle in the crown of thorns reminds us of the white-hot power of the Resurrection. Somehow in my mind I have this picture of Christ exploding out of the top of the tomb in a flash of nuclearlike energy. Talk about alternative power sources—Christ is the ultimate, inexhaustible, alternative energy source.

While this whole observance was designed for our children, I have discovered that I have gained perhaps more than they. Even those of us who think we know the true meaning of Easter need to stand at the foot of the cross with a hammer—and feel the blows.

THANKSGIVING DAY PRAYERS AT THE THOMPSONS'

Nancy gives a glimpse of how she and her family celebrate Thanksgiving:

> Our most special Thanksgiving prayers came from a surprising source. We always thought we knew what it meant to be thankful when our large extended family of aunts, uncles, cousins, and grandmothers would gather with our immediate family for a sumptuous Thanksgiving dinner. And we heartily agreed with whichever elder of the family led in the Thanksgiving table prayer, thanking God for all the blessings we all had experienced the past year. Then we would gather at the piano and sing together the 'Hallelujah Chorus' from Handel's *Messiah* to usher in the Christmas season. Yes, life was good, and we were thankful.
>
> But during our difficult years because of Dan's wrongful unemployment situation, we learned what true thankfulness really was. Our prayer at our Thanksgiving dinner was an unbelievably sincere thanksgiving.
>
> It was interesting to listen to our Cindy and Kathy pray their Thanksgiving prayers. It was no longer the usual list of thanks for Daddy and Mummy and Grandpa and Grandma. During really difficult times, children understand what real thankfulness is. Suddenly in our children's prayers, and in ours, there was a sincere appreciation for the bountiful dinner that was on our table—and deep thanks to God that He really had been the One who had supplied all our needs.

A 'THANKSGIVING TREE'

At Jan's house they begin every November 1 to focus on being thankful by getting out their 'Thanksgiving Tree.' It is a branch set in plaster of paris on which each of them daily hangs a leaf, praying thanks to God for the thing or person whose name they have written on the leaves. 'But,' says Jan, 'the thing that makes us really thankful is keeping the leaves in a bag, and getting them out the next year and seeing what God has done in answer to those prayers.'

WEDDING PRAYING FROM KURT

Kurt writes about special prayers relating to weddings:

There are many reasons to pray before and during a wedding. A wedding is the culmination of months of work, and we often pray that the day's events will occur as we have planned. Also we pray for safety in travel for the many friends and relatives who will attend. But there are two much more pressing issues to bring before the Lord in prayer.

First, a wedding may be the only time that our unsaved friends enter a church. Though we often fail to witness in our workplace or school, a wedding provides an excellent opportunity to publicly state our faith in God. We must be sure that the Gospel is clearly portrayed during the ceremony, and we should pray for the Spirit to work in the hearts of our unsaved guests. We must pray as if they had accepted an invitation to an evangelistic meeting, for so they have. A wedding is an example of an earthly groom awaiting His bride, and this can help the unsaved understand that Jesus, the Heavenly Groom, is waiting for them.

But the primary focus of our prayers is requesting God's blessings in the creation of a new entity, the marriage. When we ask for God's blessing on the marriage, we are not asking to receive health or riches or fame. We are asking for God's best for our lives, for His will. As the two should have sought His will individually, so now the couple, as one, should seek His will together. Just as Jacob wrestled with God in the night seeking as blessing, so a couple should wrestle in prayer—wrestle to turn over their preconceived plans, their selfish expectations, and their wills to the God who is all-knowing and never makes a mistake. No other preparation does so much to guarantee a successful marriage in God's eyes.

Margie and I can look back at the beginning of our life together and know that these are the prayers that we prayed—and that God is at the foundation of our union.

Kurt had been the photographer at many weddings and knew well the turmoil that precedes most ceremonies. So as he and Margie planned the preparation hours in the church leading up to their wedding, they carved out a one-half hour period for prayer. They asked all the close family, wedding party members, and officiating pastors to save that time to meet with them in a room for prayer. It was deep, moving prayer as we each prayed for the bride and groom and the ceremony. And the scheduling of that quiet time with God drew us aside from the hectic pre-wedding chaos; it quieted our hearts and invited God not only to be there but to be in control. That half hour also produced a special atmosphere of God's presence for the ceremony itself as we walked from prayer into the sanctuary. Even many guests commented on it. It was one of the most meaningful prayer times of my whole life.

WEDDINGS PRAYERS FROM CHRIS

In all of our children's marriages—Jan to Skip, Nancy to Dan, and Kurt to Margie—their father, Chris, has had the wonderful privilege of performing their ceremonies. And with that came the opportunity to pray the first prayer for each emerging couple as 'the two became one in God' in one of the most special days of their lives. *Their wedding day!*

In the thrill of adding another child to our family, and yet also in the reality of giving our child to another, Chris remembers praying this kind of prayer, from his father heart, for our children as each couple was being married:

> Dear Father, I wish I had the pen of a psalmist or the tongue of an angel that I might thank You for what You are doing. But, Father, in a very human voice I would pray that You would add the unction of Your blessing on these two. I don't pray that they would go through life without trials. Please give them enough to keep them at the foot of the cross. I do not pray that they would go through life without sorrows, but that Your presence might be their everyday companion through them. I do not pray that You would

give them great wealth, but would give them enough that they might enjoy life together.

Father, as they walk down through life, I pray that not only those around them but the two of them together honestly can say that they are walking hand in hand with their Saviour, Jesus, and because they are, all things have become more precious.

So, God, I commit them unto You, and ask that You would make out of them the kind of people that You have planned for them to be as this new couple—now one in You. In Jesus' name. Amen.

It was at our own wedding on Valentine's Day 1942 that Chris and I knelt and prayed a very special prayer. We were very aware that many of our loved ones had not received Christ as their personal Saviour yet, so we wanted to be a witness to them during our wedding ceremony as we committed ourselves to serving God throughout our marriage.

Chris' father made a three-foot high cross with soft lights on it; we covered the cross with lilies and hung it in front of our church choir loft. As we knelt under it, our soloist sang, 'Beneath the cross of Jesus, I fain would take my stand.' Although it was to declare to those present that we were taking our stand beneath the cross of Jesus, while we knelt there Chris and I prayed our own marriage commitment— to stay at the foot of Jesus' cross for the whole of our marriage.

Then fifty years later on Valentine's Day 1992, while celebrating with our whole family that special day in our lives, Chris and I once more knelt—while our family sang, 'Beneath the cross of Jesus, I fain would take my stand.'

And this is where we have been in our entire marriage— beneath the cross of Jesus. Relying on God through prayer for all our special days—and ordinary days too. *And it has worked!*

CHAPTER THIRTEEN

The Supernatural Reason
for Prayer

T HE ONLY REASON families need prayer is because there is a supernatural battle raging on earth, and human resources, wisdom, and power are not sufficient to win in this battle.

All the things that make family prayer necessary— rebellion, dissension, unforgiveness, abuse, infidelity, sickness, pain, sorrow, and eternal damnation—were brought to earth by Satan. God's world was created perfect by Him, but when Satan tempted Eve to sin in the Garden of Eden, Adam and Eve fell. This opened the door for Satan to bring all this evil to Planet Earth. And he is still the source of all of it on earth—and thus in our families.

PRAYER IS OUR SUPERNATURAL WEAPON

Since the source of all that plagues our families is supernatural, we need supernatural weapons to combat it. This is so clearly emphasized in 2 Corinthians 10:3-4:

> For though we walk in the flesh, we do not war according to

the flesh, for the weapons of our warfare are not of the flesh, but divinely powerful for the destruction of fortresses.

The only One who can bring victory over all this evil that plagues our families is God. And the way we enlist His help for our families in this supernatural battle is prayer. When we pray, God enters the supernatural problem with His supernatural wisdom and power. So our supernatural weapon is prayer (see Eph. 2:18-20).

Now it is true that God is sovereign, and He does intervene in our families' problems as He chooses, *but the only way we can enlist His help is through prayer.* Prayer is the supernatural communication to a supernatural God who then supernaturally reaches out to our families and supernaturally brings the reconciliation, healing, peace, and love our family members need.

CAN FAMILIES ESCAPE THESE EVIL ATTACKS?

Shouldn't a husband and wife who have put Christ as the head of their home be free from Satan's attacks? If they read the Bible and pray faithfully and bring up their children 'in the way they should go,' shouldn't they escape being the target of evil supernatural attacks? Not at all.

A seminary professor and his wife shared with me about their daughter who rebelled against God for two years. At times they all but lost hope of her ever coming back to God and home. 'But,' they said, 'we recognized the source of her temptation and rebellion—and *prayed and prayed spiritual warfare prayers.* And now she has come back to us, is studying at a Christian college—and has a deep relationship with the Lord!'

When Jan and Skip were first married, they were spending the night in the apartment upstairs at Grandma Moss' (my mother's) house. In the middle of the night our phone rang. 'Mother, pray! We know we are not alone up here!' I told them to claim the name and the blood of Jesus. 'We already did!' Then I said to go downstairs and get Grandma and Grandpa to pray because their prayers had tremendous spiritual power. 'We already did that too!'

Jan and Skip had done everything right and prayed everything they should. So I told them to go to bed claiming Jesus' victory over Satan. 'And,' I added, 'when you wake up in the morning, you will be amazed at the sweet peace from Jesus you will be experiencing. There will even be tears of joy in your eyes!'

The next morning Jan called again. 'You're right, Mother! There is incredible peace. If I didn't still have my robe on in which I slept all night, I wouldn't believe anything bad even happened last night!'

No one is immune from Satan's attacks. He even entered the heart of Ananias, a member of the first Christian church on earth, tempting Ananias to lie to the Holy Spirit. And he did. Also Jesus' disciple Peter, who was to become the spokesman for the early church, was sifted by Satan and so denied his Lord. Also our serving the Lord seems to make Satan more anxious to make us ineffective and defeated; or he seeks to cause us to lose our credibility if he can— because of family problems.

(A word of caution—don't blame Satan if you have brought your problems upon yourself by you or your family breaking God's laws. You then have opened yourselves up to Satan.)

WHY SPIRITUAL WARFARE SINCE THE CROSS?

Since Jesus came to defeat the works of the devil (1 John 3:8) and said on the cross, 'It is finished' (John 19:30), why are our families still plagued by the evil Satan brought to earth? Didn't Jesus fight the final battle with Satan on the cross—and didn't Jesus win? Absolutely He did! So why is there still such a huge battle with evil in our families?

The following true story illustrates clearly why the battle continues in the era in which we are living since the cross. It is a story about a python, a huge snake which grows up to twenty feet long in India and can swallow rather large animals such as a goat or sheep. It is so strong it winds itself around its live victim and squeezes to break its bones to make it easier to swallow and digest. (I brought home a newspaper article from India about a python that had swallowed a mother and her baby but spat out the mother.)

The man who told me this story is P.K. Das, the husband of my Bangalore, India, hostess. For many years Mr Das had been the United Nation's chief Asian advisor assessing their technology levels, energy systems, and productivity. I was fascinated as he told me a python experience his father had told him.

Mr Das' father had been a senior officer for the British government during British colonial rule of India early this century, travelling extensively with his entourage of servants. The British, Mr Das explained to me, had built forest houses in the jungles for their administrators to stay overnight. At one of the forest houses just south of Calcutta, a servant readying the house rushed to his father, white as a sheet and mumbling incoherently. Following him to the living room, the caretaker pointed in great agitation at a huge python coiled under a table.

So they quietly closed all the doors and windows, and his father went to check his ammunition box. He found he had just one bullet powerful enough to kill a python of that size, provided it was hit squarely in the head. So he took very careful aim, fired.

But, to his amazement, the snake did not die. Instead, it became crazed with that bullet in its head. Mr Das and his servants stood terrified outside for an hour and a half as the python violently coiled and uncoiled itself in powerful convulsions, completely smashing every piece of furniture and light fixture in the room.

Then suddenly, after that hour and a half of terror, the python crumpled to the floor and died.

'My father was quite a preacher,' Mr Das told me,

becoming the chancellor of the Serampore Theological University upon retirement. He explained the python story like this:

> Just as we had only one bullet to kill the snake, so God also had just one bullet to kill the snake, Satan. God's single bullet was His own Son Jesus Christ. Satan's head was crushed when Christ conquered him on the cross.
>
> > And the Lord God said to the serpent, 'Because you have done this, cursed are you more than all cattle....And I will put enmity between you and the woman, and between your seed and her seed [Jesus]; He shall bruise you on the head' (Gen. 3:14-15).
>
> The fatal blow, said Mr Das' father, has been dealt to the snake Satan. He has been mortally wounded already, and all the havoc and sorrow Satan now is causing on earth are only his convulsive death throes. The final end of Satan will come when Jesus comes back. It will take the second advent of Jesus for us to see the final end of Satan. The First Advent accomplished all God intended. The fatal blow was struck. But not until Jesus comes back will all of Satan's thrashing and attacking cease!

So this explains why our families are still being attacked by Satan after Jesus' victory over him on the cross. We are living in God's 'hour and a half' between the cross and Jesus' return. And Satan, crazed by the fatal wound, is violently thrashing and attacking us in the time he has left.

USING SCRIPTURE IS IMPERATIVE
Twenty-five years ago I discovered the source of so many of the problems in our family, and since then have kept up a running battle against Satan through prayer. But I have learned that it is Scripture in my praying that is so powerful against Satan. I have hurled Scripture at him as part of the Christian's armour.

> Therefore, take up the full armour of God...and the sword of the Spirit, which is the Word of God (Eph. 6:13, 17).

I have dug in my heels as I have resisted his attacks against my family.

> Submit...to God. Resist the devil, and he will flee from you (James 4:7).

I angrily have hissed through my teeth at Satan to get out when he was causing hurt and pain in my loved one.

> Be of sober spirit, be on the alert. Your adversary, the devil, prowls about like a roaring lion, seeking someone to devour. But resist him, firm in your faith (1 Peter 5:8-9).

I have enlisted the prayer support of my prayer chains and other family members according to the last item of God's armour.

> With all prayer and petition pray at all times in the Spirit, and with this in view, be on the alert with all perseverance and petition for all the saints (Eph. 6:18).

Even the Lord Jesus Himself, the actual Son of God, quoted Scripture in His Mount of Temptation forty-day battle with Satan (see Matt. 4:1-11).

CLAIMING THE NAME AND BLOOD OF JESUS

But I also learned through the years that my own name, our family name, or the name of my church or denomination had no effect on Satan. There is no power in them to fight this supernatural battle. So I have claimed the victorious name of Jesus:

> Therefore also God highly exalted Him, and bestowed on Him the name which is above every name, that at the name

of Jesus every knee should bow, of those who are in heaven, and on earth, and under the earth, and that every tongue should confess that Jesus Christ is Lord, to the glory of God the Father. (Phil. 2:9-11).

I also have claimed the irresistible power of Jesus' shed blood on Calvary against Satan:

And the great dragon was thrown down, the serpent of old who is called the devil and Satan, who deceives the whole world; he was thrown down to the earth....And they overcame him because of the blood of the Lamb and because of the word of their testimony (Rev. 12:9,11).

One day Nancy called saying, 'Mother, Cindy has developed the most horrible personality, and no matter what we do—love her more, scold her, give her more attention, or discipline her—nothing works. If we send her to her room she cries hysterically until she just about throws up. We've tried everything we can think of. *Please* pray for her!'

Five days later when calling to say goodbye as I was leaving for Italy, Nancy said, 'Mother, right after I asked you to pray for Cindy, she abruptly changed. She's the sweetest, nicest girl you ever could ask for. Absolutely the opposite of what she was. What did you pray for Cindy?'

'Nancy,' I answered, 'I went to prayer immediately. And as I was praying, God said "Satan." So I did battle with Satan, claiming the blood of Jesus in the name of Jesus.'

The next day in Italy, during my devotional Bible reading I read this reassuring verse about Jesus' power over evil in Luke 4:36:

For with authority and power He [Jesus] commands the unclean spirits, and they come out.

After returning from Italy, I said to Nancy, 'I won't always be available to pray, so it's imperative that you learn what to pray in these situations.' Sensing her hesitancy, I said, 'Honey, I don't like this subject either. In fact, I hate it. But it's extremely important that the family's elder members know how to pray scripturally claiming the blood and name of Jesus, and to experientially know the power Christians have over Satan and his cohorts. With the victorious Jesus living in you, you can have an unshakable attitude of authority over Satan—lived in front of your children in all the hassles of Satan.'

CLEANSING OUR HOME

Satan attacks our family by bringing confusion, defensiveness, oppression, and a heavy negative feeling into the atmosphere of our home. Frequently, I struggle under these attacks for a period of time before I wake up to the source. Then I immediately address Satan, telling him in the name of Jesus to get out of our house. Then, after asking God to cleanse the house with the blood of Jesus, I ask Him to fill it with Himself—all His purity and positive qualities. And it works. But it is amazing how often this happens, especially when I am working on material that threatens Satan. But I know the source—and what to do about it!

A few days ago while writing this chapter, I began feeling many of those things. Just then Skip called, and he prayed over the phone asking God to cleanse our house, claiming the blood and name of Jesus. It is hard to describe what I felt, but it was as if something lifted, and the air seemed to be so clear—like water after impurities have been removed.

SKIP'S SPIRITUAL WARFARE

Our son-in-law Skip has discovered God's power over Satan's influence in their own home. Here are some of his own thoughts:

> We came across a church liturgy several years ago which was inspiring to use as various members in our church 'agape group' moved into new homes. We would all walk through the various rooms in the house, even stopping in the

boiler room, and in each room give a short Bible reading or Bible verse and pray. As we cleansed each room with God's Word and prayer, we believe we made a declaration in the heavenlies that only God's purposes, presence, and Spirit were permitted in this new house.

Last year as we made preparations for Easter, I decided to construct a cross for our home. The chain saw hummed, and soon a six-foot cross lay before me. Hammering nails to erect it, I was overcome by emotion at the thought that my sin required a cross to be constructed for Jesus to be crucified. With tears in my eyes and the cross I had made on my shoulder, I brought it into the house. I was greeted by an outburst of crying by my three children, even including three-month-old Brett. We sensed an evil source to the cries, and were able to pray, allowing God to remove the foreign influence from our Easter and restore peace to them.

Our bedtime ritual with our children is a high point of our day. Drawing our children into our arms, we ask for prayer requests or items of praise. As we deal with the specific requests, we make a point to enclose our children in *God's cocoon of protection*. We ask for *His angels* to be present in their protective role. We ask for *God's hedge of protection* to be established around us and the *blood of Jesus* to be applied to us. Standing in His might, as believers in Jesus Christ, we *take authority over Satan and his kingdom* and *rebuke it in Jesus' name*. We ask that *Satan's purposes and plan* for us be cancelled and rebuked, and in its place *God's purposes and plan* be allowed to happen.

Occasionally, perhaps about 2 a.m., we hear a thud and the staccato patter of little feet. One of our children announces a 'scary dream' and cuddles up to us, asking 'Daddy, please pray that my scary dream will go away.' It is a father's richest blessing to sense the tenseness and fear dissolve as God always answers that prayer.

STAYING ON THE VICTORY SIDE

Always stay on the victory side in your praying. Never question who is stronger, Jesus or Satan. Jesus always has been God, Satan just a created being. And never succumb to the lie that Satan might win. There is nothing in the

Ephesians 6 'armour' section that even hints at falling, only standing—*if* we follow God's rules and wear His spiritual armour.

The first time I recall praying a very important spiritual warfare prayer was for my teenage Nancy in the early 1970s. She finally told me that for years she had had dreams of a terrifying face in a mirror telling her that in some way she was the heir of England's Bloody Mary. Feeling like a mother whose child had been attacked by a mad dog, I rushed into the battle without really knowing too much about what I was doing. But I seated us both by our dining room table, and then prayed claiming the blood of Jesus in the name of Jesus until we felt the victory come. I used every Scripture I could think of, swinging away with the 'sword of the Spirit'. I was too furious to be afraid. Too incensed to be cautious.

But it worked. After that praying, Nancy told me that face appeared in her mirror only once more—pale and indistinct and as if in a cracked mirror. It told her it could not come back any more. And it didn't!

The greatest thing of all is that God not only delivered from those horrible attacks, but now has erased it completely from Nancy's mind. And I too have never been haunted by it, and had to refer to the notes I wrote at the time to make sure of the correct details for this book. *Victory in Jesus!*

Another thing that routs Satan is praise music. I frequently rock in a chair on my deck singing 'In the name of Jesus, In the name of Jesus, I have the victory—and Satan will have to flee!' And I love to sit at my piano playing with gusto and finality, 'There's power in the blood—of the Lamb.' When in the midst of the battle, I find myself singing—in the car, in the kitchen, at the office, or wherever I am—the chorus based on the Scripture on which I firmly stand—1 John 4:4:

> Greater is He [Jesus] that is in you, than he [Satan] that is in the world (AV).

Skip told me of their use of praise tapes. 'Our home has been said by many to be "so peaceful.' We do believe that God "inhabits the praises of His people' (Ps. 22:3, NKJV). We have a large collection of praise music which frequently is playing. For several years Jenna had a special praise tape which she went to sleep listening to. Singing praises with our children in the car,' says Skip, 'the miles are shorter and our lives are enriched by the unity of His Spirit.'

Many times I have stepped into Skip and Jan's house with praise music charging the atmosphere with God's presence. Satan cannot stand against songs of God's praise and Jesus' victory.

MINISTRY-RELATED ATTACKS OF SATAN

In 1972 I started teaching in youth groups, schools, and colleges on the dangers of the occult experimenting our young people were practising; and I experienced wonderful protection and peace from God because of the praying of my 'occult prayer chain'. However, a local pastor who found Jesus after coming out of a childhood home with incredible occult power said to me, 'Evelyn, I believe you will be strong enough to stand up to Satan, but where he will get to you is through attacking your children. You as a mother will find it very difficult to battle him at the expense of your own children.' And I have found this to be very true.

Our Nancy says she always knows when the Lord is moving with special effectiveness in my ministry, because at that time she and husband, Dan, always experience unusual hassles in their family. For years, she told me, they mentally kept track of this, and finally were convinced it was more than coincidence. 'It usually isn't one big thing,' Nancy said, 'although at times it is, but a series of extremely upsetting things you just know will never happen—but they do. Most are not life-threatening but are beyond the normal hassles of life. But their sheer numbers necessitate expending so much time on them, and focuses my energy away from the important things in my life. And they contribute significantly to anxiety, and sometimes just routine life becomes a challenge.

'Also,' Nancy continued, 'they seem to have a pattern, always coming when God is blessing your prayer ministry. Dan and I now believe strongly that they are not from God, but from Satan because he wants to dilute your ministry's effectiveness. So I have named them "hassle demons".'

'But,' said Nancy, 'those hassles produced an incredible benefit at our house. Whichever child was being affected, we would pray and pray together. When one of us parents would feel at the end of our rope, we learned to trust God in a new way in those very difficult situations.'

Yes, it is very hard on my mother-heart even to surmise that my ministry could cause spiritual hassles in my children. And I have prayed much about this through the years. Many times I have discussed this with Dan and Nancy, and over and over have asked them if they wanted me to give up my ministry. But I am overwhelmed and humbled at their unselfishness and the sacrifice they are willing to make for God's will to be done. Their resounding answer to this question always is, 'No! We will pay any price we need to pay!'

My board and I have noticed the correlation also. Whenever I am going to a new continent, publishing a new book, or some other first related to my ministry, not only do my family and I feel the unusually strong attacks from Satan, but they do too. They even report their families falling apart at the same time. And our families' hassles take up so much of our time, energy, and praying that our time of praying for our ministry is drastically diminished. It is like the thwarting of Satan that Paul experienced when he wanted to go once to Thessalonica (see 1 Thes. 2:18).

When my first prayer tape was published, our youngster Kurt sighed a big sigh of relief. 'Now maybe I'll be able to sleep nights, Mother.' And Jan, away at college, would frequently call and say, 'I know what you spoke on tonight,

Mother!' And she was always right—spiritual warfare. The last time I returned from India, Nancy said, 'Mother, lots of souls were being won in India, weren't they?' I said yes, why? 'Because of the hassle we have been going through here!'

Reading James 1:1-4 on February 14, 1990, about trials believers experience, I recorded, 'Finished writing *Battling the Prince of Darkness* book today. I have had complete joy through the whole writing since July '89. But the hassles from Satan have come from attacks on my family, keeping me off balance and consumed by praying for them.' Satan's attacks on my family have been the hardest of all spiritual battles for me.

BOXING WINDMILLS?

One night Jenna and Crista were sleeping in their favourite 'cosy' of blankets and pillows on the floor on either side of Chris' and my bed. Suddenly in the middle of the night Chris reared up in bed and bellowed, 'Get out of here, you…you…you…!' While he boxed wildly at a white object seemingly floating in the air in the darkened room, two sleepy heads popped up over the sides of the bed and gaped in bewilderment.

But when we turned on the light we saw it was only a white terrycloth robe somebody had hung by its hood like a head over the closet door—with its sleeves at a rakish angle like arms. We all had a good laugh, and settled in for the rest of the night's sleep.

I wish all battles in our home were only like Don Quixote boxing windmills. I wish they all were with an imaginary enemy like that. But, unfortunately, they are real battles with a real supernatural being—who has chosen our families as one of his main, and most productive, battlegrounds for his evil, diabolical plans.

* * *

A CONCLUDING WORD—PONDERING OR PRAYING?

Much of what we think is prayer actually is only pondering. Even when we are on our knees in our prayer closets, it is easy just to roll our own thoughts and our own answers around in our minds, not really including God at all. This is not prayer; it is only pondering.

My dictionary defines 'ponder' like this: 'To consider something deeply and thoroughly; to meditate over or upon, to weigh carefully in the mind; to consider thoughtfully; to reflect, cogitate, deliberate, ruminate.' This is a healthy process as it helps us sort out whys, unravel perplexing puzzles, come to conclusions, and even put to rest hurtful events. But people frequently think they have prayed when they have spent time pondering. *Pondering is not prayer*. Only when we involve God in this process does it turn into prayer.

In the supernatural battle for our families, pondering is inadequate. It is powerless to change the family problem about which we are deliberating.

In pondering we only wallow in our own reactions and feelings with all of our human biases and misunderstandings in control. At best pondering can give us human answers to our dilemmas which may or may not be right. There is no divine guidance or wisdom introduced into the family need.

But when we include God, our pondering suddenly involves the omniscient, all-wise God of the universe. The God who never makes a mistake. The God who knows all the whys, all the outcomes, all the perfecting He intends through everything that happens to our families. When God becomes personally involved in our pondering, there are accurate conclusions and correct attitudes in and for our families—supplied by a loving, caring, all-knowing God.

When our pondering turns to praying, we also have the divine input of the omnipotent, all-powerful God of heaven, who has the power to intervene supernaturally into our family problems. And He also desires to supply us with all the power we need to cope with, handle, and solve our family needs.

Only when we include God in our ponderings are we praying.

Examine carefully what you have been calling your 'prayertime'. How much of it is really praying? Have you learned to address God deliberately—and then listen to His responses? Or are you basically just pondering? Make sure!

> Draw near to God, and He will draw near to you (James 4:8).

Then heaven will open up to you, and God on His throne will attune His ear to you—eager to provide all of Himself to you and your family—because you prayed!